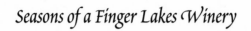

Seasons of a Finger Lakes Winery

Seasons of a
FINGER LAKES WINERY

JOHN C. HARTSOCK

CORNELL UNIVERSITY PRESS

Ithaca & London

First published 2011 by Cornell University Press

Printed in the United States of America

Library of Congress Cataloging-in-Publication Data

Hartsock, John C., 1951–
    Seasons of a Finger Lakes winery / John C. Hartsock.
        p. cm.
    Includes bibliographical references.
    ISBN 978-0-8014-4881-2 (cloth: alk. paper)
    1. Long Point Winery (Aurora, N.Y.)   2. Wineries—New York (State)—Finger Lakes Region.   3. Vintners—New York (State)—Finger Lakes Region.   4. Wine and wine making—New York (State)—Finger Lakes Region.   I. Title.
    HD9379.L66H37   2011
    338.7'663200974768—dc22   2010049858

Cornell University Press strives to use environmentally responsible suppliers and materials to the fullest extent possible in the publishing of its books. Such materials include vegetable-based, low-VOC inks and acid-free papers that are recycled, totally chlorine-free, or partly composed of nonwood fibers. For further information, visit our website at www.cornellpress.cornell.edu.

Cloth printing   10 9 8 7 6 5 4 3 2 1

For our son Peter,
the fruit of the vine

CONTENTS

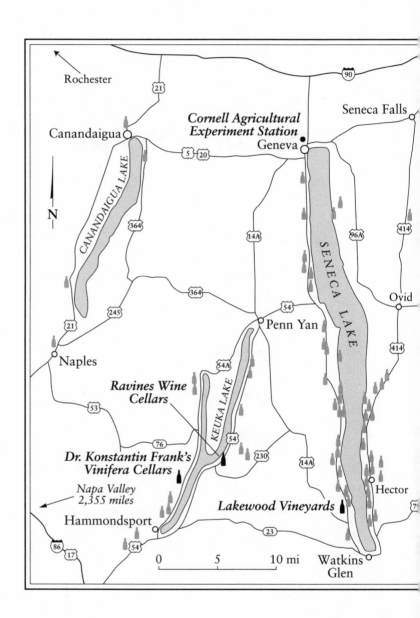

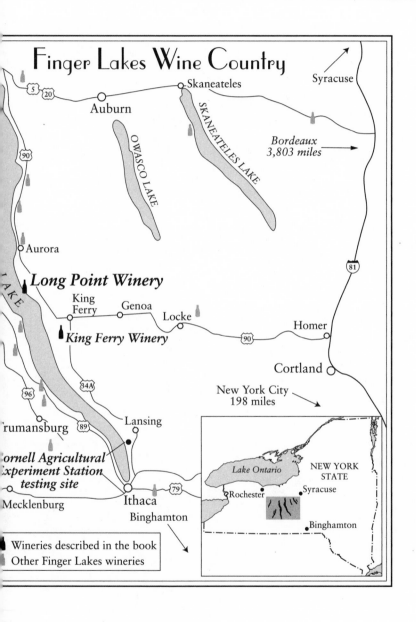

Finger Lakes Wine Country

Syracuse

Skaneateles

Auburn

O W A S C O   L A K E

S K A N E A T E L E S   L A K E

Bordeaux
3,803 miles

81

Aurora

Long Point Winery

King
Ferry

Genoa

Locke

Homer

King Ferry Winery

90

Cortland

New York City
198 miles

Lansing

rumansburg   89

ornell Agricultural
xperiment Station
testing site

96

34A

Mecklenburg

Ithaca

79

Binghamton

Lake Ontario

NEW YORK
STATE

Rochester

Syracuse

Binghamton

Wineries described in the book
Other Finger Lakes wineries

5   20

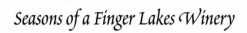

Seasons of a Finger Lakes Winery

WINTER

THROUGH THE SWIRL OF SNOW you could just make out in the distance the rows of leafless grapevines stitching across the hillside. Nearby, a snow devil twisted in a churning cloud amid whiteouts blanketing the neighboring farm field. Still farther, the dark outline of Cayuga Lake was a shadow lost in the snowstorm sweeping out of Canada.

Hardly a promising day for making wine, I thought.

Inside Long Point Winery the only evidence of the snowstorm was the distant muffled snap of the "Open" flag outside, beckoning futilely in the wind.

One thing was clear: Gary would have few customers for wine tastings today.

Gary Barletta was oblivious to the storm as he leaned over and the fluorescent light flashed across his balding head before he poked it between rows of oak barrels reflecting a tawny color in the light. He wrapped his hand around a large bung—a cork-like plug—in a bottom barrel, twisted, and withdrew it.

The owner of—and more important the winemaker at—Long Point put his nose up to the wine in the barrel and drew in deeply, slowly, his gray luminescent eyes intently focused.

"I like the way this is coming along," he said.

He took a wine thief—a suction dropper—and inserted it into the bunghole, withdrawing a small quantity of Chardonnay. He filled first one wine glass and then another a quarter full, holding both by the stems between the fingers of his curled fist. The aging wine reflected a pale, transparent gold.

He extended his hand to me and offered a glass.

It was harsh in the nose.

"It's still young," he said, reading my mind.

He paused as he continued to draw in the nose. "It could be more complex." He paused again. "It needs more oak." Staring into the distance, he thought about it. "But it's coming along. I like it better than last year's." And that surprised me given how much he had sung the praises of the previous year's Chardonnay, as if it were a father's cherished first born.

If there was nothing else to drink, one could probably drink this new Chardonnay, and that's how it must have been for thousands of years past when most wine drinkers drank their wine young before it could turn to vinegar. Only someone who has spent season after season nurturing wine could detect how this raw new wine would age slowly into something more illuminating.

Gary picked up a stainless steel stirring paddle, a right-angled handle with a small paddle at the end of it. He inserted it in the bunghole, and slowly, quietly began to row back and forth, back and forth.

The paddle stirred up the lees—the sediment—to impart flavor. The lees had settled in the barrel since Gary last stirred two weeks ago. He continued silently paddling the Chardonnay, pushing and pulling against the volume of wine resisting the paddle blade in the sixty-gallon barrel. You could hear a cricket, a refugee from the storm, saw his fiddle, it was so quiet in the winery.

On a winter's day that's how you can often find Gary. Testing. Teasing. Hoping.

To a non-wine drinker there might appear to be something slightly illicit in wanting to start your own winery. After all, it doesn't contribute to the basic necessities of life such as clothing, shelter, the greater public weal. When you think about it, starting a winery appears to be downright self-indulgent. Which may explain why Gary's wife, Rosemary, likes to say, sometimes with a hint of embarrassment, that the winery was Gary's idea.

"I'm doing it to humor him."

But that's not entirely true. Because while Rosie is the kind of person who doesn't let on at first, she is as passionately committed to the winery as Gary. For example, when I told her one day that the Robert Mondavi Winery in California had been sold to the largest wine company in the world, she said, "I wouldn't sell. No matter what they offered me."

Not that Constellation Brands, which bought Mondavi in 2004, would take note of a little mom-and-pop operation like the Barletta's. But to Rosie it was the principle of the thing. They had worked too hard to get to the point where they are now: They had built a winery. *Their* winery.

Then there is the matter of palate. Ask Gary. Because in many ways, Rosie's palate is just as refined as Gary's when it comes to tasting wine. She will tell him when she thinks the wine is not good.

"And you know, she's usually right," he admits.

Once again, to her it's the principle of the thing: "We are not going to sell bad wine." At least not knowingly, because there are times when wine can take on a life of its own, times when it can turn unpalatable, even into a monster, defying the best efforts of the winemaker.

A few miles south of the college hamlet of Aurora in Upstate New York, Long Point Winery is located in—and indeed defined by—what is called the Finger Lakes, a region of eleven lakes created by glaciation and stretching like the fingers of a hand. Cayuga Lake, the longest at a little over 38 miles, sits in a valley below the Barletta's winery. The region, some 70 miles east to west, and 50 miles north to south in the central portion of the state, is often characterized as the "Finger Lakes Wine Country" because it has ninety bonded wineries, making it one of the highest concentrations of wineries in any one area outside of California.

Gary and Rosie opened their winery in 1999, after years of dreaming and planning and dreaming...and more dreaming. And yet their experience is not unusual because they are part of a phenomenon that has taken place across the United States in recent years: the rise of *craft* or *artisanal* or *boutique* wineries, as they are variously called, springing up at an almost maddening pace and motivated by a passion for wine. There is now at least one winery in every state, even in such unlikely places as Maine, North Dakota, and Alaska. (The latter has eight.) Often they are founded by wine enthusiasts who work other jobs during the week and stir the lees or man the tasting counters on weekends, like Gary and Rosie. Until he semiretired a few years ago, Gary worked at the hospital in Cortland some twenty-nine miles and a world away from the Finger Lakes wine country and culture. He is a nuclear medicine technician by profession and occasionally still puts in a few hours in the morning. His boss is Rosie.

"She's the boss there. She's the boss here," he likes to say.

Only, when you get to know them, you can't be so sure.

Rosie runs the business end of the winery. With smooth features and calm, feline eyes, she conveys a content self-possession—like a cat's—when you first meet her. But there's another side that she doesn't often reveal: She can be vulnerable, working her nine-to-five as the director of imaging and cardiology at the hospital, then manning the tasting counter and doing the winery books on weekends. And she and Gary are grandparents. Like many baby boomers on the other side of the second half of their lives, they are now realizing the blessings of what they have accomplished, and then some. Caught between demands, there are days when Rosie's calmness and self-possession can give way to panic. That's when she says of this winery business, "I'm doing it to humor Gary."

But again, you can't be so sure.

"I only wish I had done this ten years earlier," Gary said one day not long after we met several years ago. He was pumping Chardonnay out of oak barrels into large, white plastic holding tanks. As he spoke his eyes gestured at the white oak barrels stacked in receding rows across the winery.

Although the wine calories were beginning to take their toll on his midriff now that he had reached his mid-fifties, Gary's body still betrayed the gymnast's sinuous physique from his college years. He puts a positive spin on the fact that he's balding; there's "less shingles on the roof," he says, and then he reminds you that Robert Mondavi, the great impresario of American wine, was also bald. "So maybe there's hope for me."

Typical Gary blarney. And he is half Irish. But his roots remain firmly in the old Italian neighborhood on the north side of Syracuse in the part of New York State that can be more Midwest than East Coast because people still go to church and barbershops close at 5 p.m. In a photo of Gary from when he was about eight years old, one taken in the old Italian neighborhood, he has the waifish look of an Italian shepherd boy from the hills of Bari in southern Italy, the region his winemaking grandfather Dominic left when he came to America during the first decade of the twentieth century. Now that Gary had reached middle age and the balding pate, he had fully embraced the family passion for making wine. With his firm nose and closely trimmed salt-and-pepper beard, his visage reminded me of a profile on an old Roman coin, perhaps Hadrian, gnarled and scruffy from the campaigns defending the borders of his empire. All Gary needed was a crown of laurel—or vine—leaves.

Syracuse is where Gary picked up what could pass for street smarts; he's someone who's not afraid to be in your face—but then the Roman emperors were often street brawlers, too, before they donned the imperial purple. Yet there are times when another Gary emerges. That's when he repeats once more what has become a refrain: "Yeah, I would say that is my only regret: I wish I had done this ten years earlier."

And as he spoke he looked up from a glass demijohn he was filling with Chardonnay and had the earnest look of someone who suddenly has insight into the profoundest of cosmic mysteries. That's when, despite the street smarts, you realize he is still capable of innocence.

After observing Gary and Rosie make wine over the course of nearly a decade, I have more questions than when I began. I am not a wine expert. I am just another student of the fruit of the vine trying to understand its mysteries. I can tell what I like and what I don't, and Gary and Rosie have taught me much about many of the finer qualities. Yet I still often feel I am a novice. Wine is that complicated, if not confounding. Of course, I know my palate is not as refined as theirs. But, and it's an important *but*, they are like most wine lovers, eager to share the knowledge and the enthusiasm of what they love and how it is made. That's why I started dropping by the winery, and so began my education in wine and its making.

Today, after ten years in business, the winery has seen many changes. Gary started in 1999 with no vines. Now he has eight acres—one and a half of Chardonnay, a little over one acre of Cabernet Franc, one and a half of Pinot Gris, and nearly three and a half of Riesling. Meanwhile, Joe Shevalier, Gary's first vineyard manager who taught me so much about the vines, has moved over to nearby King Ferry Winery. Dan Stevens is now vineyard manager at Long Point, and he has continued my education. And there has been a momentous shift for Gary, slow to be sure but as inexorable as the shifting of the continental plates: Starting out a confirmed red wine man and maker, he has moderated, even mellowed, so that the man whose whites his wife once said "suck," has become increasingly a white wine man, one who now cherishes the nuances of whites in a way he had not before because he has grown the grapes on his own land, in his own vineyard, in their own time.

Yet, there is also an unchanging quality to the passage of the seasons at a winery like theirs. This is because their efforts, I discover, are part of a cycle that goes back unbroken to before recorded time. As Rosie put it prosaically one day—this was their seventh year in business—"It's just the same old ritual." In the incantation of "the same old ritual" and the ongoing changes is to be found, I discover, a paradox. On the one hand, Gary and Rosie measure out their lives according to the steady unfolding of the cultivation of the vine and the making of the wine. On the other, they always face the unexpected as they struggle year after year to bring in the best crop they can despite the fickleness of nature and to nurture the fruit into the best wine man and nature can contrive in a relationship that is not always cordial.

Which leaves one to wonder: Does the wine make the man?

It begins at a time of year modest in ambition.

When winter starts its slow decline but spring is still more a distant memory than a season to anticipate, and when those Upstaters who can afford to flee the seemingly endless months of gray clouds for the sun of Florida, Gary's vineyard manager plans, without much in the way of fanfare, to do the bud checks.

In the Finger Lakes one morning in late February, much of the snow had blown off the land but patches still remained in the farm fields, stray pieces to a winter's puzzle. While some of the snow had melted, most had been picked up by the winter-long winds, blowing it east into the deep stream valleys in the highlands to the Appalachians.

Joe Shevalier could only hazard a guess as to what he would find in the vineyard. But he prepared for the worst.

"Now we'll find out how bad it really is," he said. He pulled on his down coat and donned his green Long Point Winery baseball cap.

Joe was forty-nine, with a bristle moustache and chestnut hair that hinted at Scotsman red. He tugged on his gloves and picked up a white five-gallon plastic bucket. He walked out the side door of the winery, the one to the small laboratory where through the course of the year Gary engages in the alchemy that nurtures grapes and refines wine.

Outside the temperature was in the mid-thirties—warm for this time of year. But the ground was still icy in places and soft from the melt in others. Joe walked down to the vineyard, across bare patches of frozen grass brown from the winter cloud cover when cold air blowing out of the Canadian Arctic picks up moisture from Lake Ontario—what in Upstate is called the "lake effect." The gate gave a shrill cry on the hinges as he entered the world of the vineyard. There, the vines presented a tangle of brown-and-gray coarse-barked trunks and smooth-barked canes depending on their age, with little to indicate the future harvest.

This year the snow between the Chardonnay rows wasn't too deep.

"You should have seen last year. It was up to my thighs," Joe said. He turned down between the first and second rows of vines.

He stopped a third of the way down the first row and set the bucket in the snow. He reached out and took a cane in hand, examining. He looked for canes with close to fifteen buds, or, more properly, *nodes*. Each node is a shallow pea-sized bump that contains three buds. His index finger started levitating above the nodes, counting, moving silently up the cane. Nineteen nodes. He wrapped his vine clippers

around the crotch where cane and trunk met, and squeezed, clipping through the pencil-thick cane. The cane dangled, suspended and ensnared among the branches. Joe plucked it out, then clipped off the last four nodes so he would have his fifteen-node sample. He placed the cane in the bucket.

Joe retraced his footsteps in the snow. He walked around to the next row and two-thirds of the way down its length. He found a cane, clipped it, and removed the excess nodes.

He cut one cane from each of the twenty-four rows. When he finished he walked up to the Cabernet Franc vineyard, to the small section initially planted as an experiment to see if Cab Franc could grow there, and cut two canes. He wrapped the two canes together with a black twisty tie to separate them from the Chardonnay and deposited them in the white bucket.

Back at the winery, he picked up the cold water hose, turned it on, and filled the white bucket a quarter full. The canes would spend the next few days warming up and absorbing the water.

Three days later Joe arrived early in the morning. He entered the gloom of the winery lit by the meager light allowed by the heavy gray blanket of clouds outside through the garage door windows. Even when he turned on the fluorescents the light was desultory, leaving in dim shadows the stacked wine barrels, the stainless steel storage tanks, and the corrugated cardboard boxes of bottled wines stacked almost to the ceiling.

Now he would know if there would be a crop in the upcoming year. Not that the winery would live or die by it because Gary also buys grapes from other growers. But at stake was the psychological investment.

Joe turned on the lamp atop the folding table that serves as Gary's office just outside the testing lab. Maneuvering between buckets and glass demijohns, he grasped the white plastic bucket containing the canes and placed it on the floor at the end of the table. Joe sat down in an old oak swivel chair, pulled the Chardonnay canes out of the bucket and laid them across the table. He pulled his eyeglasses out of his shirt pocket and put them on, pushing them up against the bridge of his nose.

The canes had had three days to warm up, drawing on the water in the bucket to swell the living buds in the fifty-five-degree warmth of the winery. Joe picked up a Chardonnay cane and laid it under the lamplight. He took a single-edged Red Devil razor blade and pressed down on the cane with the fingers of his left hand just above the first node.

"Sometimes you know they are dead because it has the fuzzy," Joe said. What he meant was that the surface of the node had developed a gray fuzz. This past winter temperatures rose to sixty in December. The buds were tricked into thinking it was spring and began to stir from their winter sleep. The fuzz was an indicator that the nodes were beginning to bud.

"Then the cold hit us."

That's not the case now as Joe drew the blade across the base of the node, slicing through the soft bark so that it fell away in a flesh-like flake.

Under a magnifying glass in the light of the lamp, Joe examined. A grape node has primary, secondary, and tertiary buds. The primary bud on this first node was evenly round, a sixteenth of an inch in diameter. It was a moist, luminescent green, like a spring lawn glittering in the sunshine after a downpour. It was healthy and revealed the life contained deep in the vines that otherwise presented such a doleful aspect at this time of year.

"That's what I like to see," Joe said, examining the speck of green in the magnifying glass.

The secondary bud was a much smaller, irregular oblong clinging to the side of the primary, only just visible to the naked eye. The secondary bud is part of the grapevine's survival strategy. If the primary bud dies, then the secondary bud can still bear a few grapes, although their quality is not as good as those of the primary. It, too, was green. Finally, there was the tertiary bud, just a faint speck even under the magnifying glass and located at the edge of the primary bud, opposite the secondary. It doesn't bear grapes, only leaves, but that's all that's needed for the vine to survive for another year.

Joe wrote down the condition of the buds on a sheet of paper laid out in a grid.

Then he sliced through another node and a sliver of node-flesh fell away. He inspected under the magnifying glass, his brow furrowing above his eyeglasses, which had slid down his nose.

"Primary's dead on this one. But the others are okay."

The primary was black, a telltale sign. But the others were green. Then he moved to the next node.

He examined more than 350 nodes on the twenty-four Chardonnay canes, one cane for each row in the vineyard. He recorded the condition of each bud—either they're green and living or black and dead—to create the sample. Then he did the Cab Franc.

When he completed the survey, the results weren't as bad as he feared, given the dire warnings. Or at least they weren't as bad as what he had heard other vineyards had experienced.

"It could have been worse," Joe said as he looked over his grid. The kill rate for the primary nodes was about 4 percent. And the Cabernet Franc canes were fine, although two canes hardly made for a satisfactory sample.

Gary attributed the low kill rate to his location: He's on the east side of Cayuga Lake and the prevailing winds come out of the west and northwest. Cayuga is the last of the biggest fingers in the succession of lakes. As the winter winds travel over the combined microclimates of Canandaigua, Keuka, Seneca, and Cayuga lakes, the air warms up.

"I've never understood why there are so many wineries on the west side of Cayuga, and only King Ferry Winery and Long Point on the east. We get the moderating influence," Gary said in the early years. Since then, however, others have seen the virtues of his side of the lake and it now has five wineries.

Of course, bud damage varies from year to year. Some years there's virtually no damage in the vineyard. But on rare occasion it can get to minus ten or even twenty degrees Fahrenheit in the dead of winter, and the damage can be extensive.

Still, Joe's relief at the findings was subdued. In the seasons ahead there will be challenges and potentially disastrous circumstances over which he has little control. "We'll see," he said—of the same old ritual.

Some seasons the outlook is not so promising. On a weekend in late February one year, when Upstate was locked in a perpetual glaze of snow and ice, Gary and Joe attended a conference near Geneva, which sits at the top of neighboring Seneca Lake. The conference is hosted every year by the Cornell Cooperative Extension's Finger Lakes Grape Program. This is the time of year, late winter, when the winemaker and the vineyardist, driven by some pagan foreboding, look for portents in everything. And it wasn't looking good.

Although there were presentations on myriad topics, such as downy mildew, cane borers, and fertilizer and pesticide applications, everyone came to find out just how bad the bud damage was from early January freezes. Actually, they came looking more for hope, because the early results were already coming in from the vineyards. In some cases there appeared to be 90 percent bud kill. That meant most of the coming season's crop had been lost, at least a crop of any size and quality.

In the breezeway to the entrance of the Holiday Inn John Balliet, the vineyard manager at King Ferry Winery, smiled cheerfully, taking a drag on a cigarette.

"I don't think I'll have to prune this year. I just have to wait to see what survived." And he was still smiling, cheerfully, as if it were all a big joke.

Later, Joe said, "Maybe I won't have to prune this year. We'll see if we have any crop."

Gary smiled wryly at the irony of not having to prune because he lost most of his buds.

"I'll tell you, it's so bad, maybe I'll have to start thinking about building a nursing home. That's where the money is," he said, because recently he had to place his elderly mother in a nursing home.

"January was one of the coldest in the past fifty years," reported Tim Martinson, who at the time ran the grape program before moving on to head the state's Viticulture Extension Program at the Agricultural Experiment Station in Geneva. "We can expect winter injury to be extensive, particularly on the most sensitive *Vitis vinifera*—growers have been reporting 50 to 95 percent primary bud injury on Chardonnay, and somewhat less on Riesling."

As for what survived on the vines, Martinson made the common refrain official: "It may be a good year to prune lightly during the dormant season, seeing what pushes up, and adjusting shoot number after bud burst. You can always remove more shoots, but you can't put them back on the vine."

So much for hope.

"I've already contracted for grapes from Long Island," Pete Saltonstall, the owner of King Ferry, told me. "I want to get it in writing this week."

A little later, over a lunch of baked chicken à la Holiday Inn, stringy and fat, the gloomy talk continued.

"We may not have to prune at all," said Mike Countryman, the vineyard manager at Casa Larga Vineyards near Rochester. And like the others he's half joking, half serious. It's as if in the half measures they can avoid their own vulnerability to the whims of nature.

Given the overall gloom at the February conference, there was little else to do but taste wine. All the wineries brought samples, and the wine tasting of the fruit of good years was a welcome escape from the doubtful prospects of the year to come. Gary traded in his hat as a winemaker and played the role of wine taster, tasting his competitors' wines.

When he inhaled the nose of a Chardonnay, his gray eyes shifted and darted. He seemed to be searching for some ulterior motive. He lifted the glass and inhaled a second time, and there was a quizzical look, as he tried to puzzle out some mystery. Finally, he lifted the glass to his lips and drank. The glass paused at his mouth, forgotten, hanging suspended.

"This lacks body," he said. "And there's a little bit of vinegar." He was whispering, because it wasn't polite to criticize your fellow winemakers in public.

A little later, he said of another wine, "I like this. It has good fruit."

Joe suggested they try the 2002 Cabernet Franc from the Knapp Winery, where Gary had been buying his Cabernet Franc grapes until his own were mature enough for harvesting.

Could he be objective?

"Absolutely," Gary said.

The server poured a small tasting. Gary picked up the glass and inhaled deeply from the rim. His eyes moved across the floor, then the walls, then back down to the floor, taking in the circuit of the wine taster's universe. He lingered longer on the nose than the taste. When he raised his glass and sipped, his survey of the universe was more circumscribed, more concise. Immediately he knew the answer to his search in his taste buds.

"I think this is better than my Cabernet Franc," he said, thinking of last year's vintage. "But I think my Cab Franc for this year is better."

He had not bottled that vintage yet. His vintage from the year before was on the table at the conference. But since he wasn't comparing the same vintages—a season's vintage can vary considerably—it was faint praise for his competitor.

Was he really being objective?

"Absolutely." Then he added, "But I don't know. When I filter and bottle mine, I may strip away some of the flavor. Then we'll see." Always, the weighing, the attempting to tease out nuance.

Later, I noticed that no one was spitting—the not very pleasant habit of the professional taster so he or she won't become drunk from so many tastings.

"Yeah, no one's spitting," Joe observed.

"No, no one's spitting," Gary echoed.

I wasn't either, but spitting was not a habit I had acquired yet.

Gary grinned sheepishly as he finished his flight. Given the bud damage and that no one will have to prune this year, why bother?

All of which makes one wonder, why do it? Upstate New York does not have California's notoriously perfect growing conditions. But

California's wines were once considered rather pedestrian until the Judgment of Paris, the famous wine competition in 1976 in which, in a blind tasting, French wine judges selected California wines as the best in a group of French and California wines.

Part of understanding what the Barlettas and others like them are doing is to understand what has happened to the wine industry in the United States in recent years.

"It's just been an explosion," says Bill Nelson of the growth of small wineries. A silver-haired, soft-spoken man, Nelson was, at the time, executive director of WineAmerica in Washington, D.C., which represents the interests of the wine industry, large and small.

During an initial growth spurt between 1995 and 2005, the number of taxpaying wineries—meaning those that sell to the public—more than doubled in the United States, from 1,817 to 3,820. By 2008 there were more than 5,600, according to Nelson. That has meant a growth rate of more than 300 percent since 1995. Some 43 percent of the wineries were founded in California during this period. But the rest were started in the other states. This is a national phenomenon, then, not just a California fad. And the vast majority of wineries are small craft operations like Long Point. They qualify as craft or artisanal wineries because their production is small and every vintage is unique. However, one should not equate craft wines necessarily with high quality wines. Craft wineries can make wines that run the gamut. But there is no effort to make wine as many of the big producers do, predictable, often uninspiring, but also without pretense.

One approximate measure for what constitutes a craft winery is the production of less than 25,000 cases of wine a year: Those wineries accounted for the majority, or some 72 percent, of wineries in the United States in 2004. That's 1,801 out of 2,481 wineries, according to WineAmerica data up to that year. It's into this group that Long Point falls. The Barlettas bottle from 4,200 to 4,500 cases of wine a year.

Using 25,000 cases as a cutoff for what constitutes a craft winery may be imprecise but it is useful because only 23 percent of American wineries produced between 25,000 and 250,000 cases in 2004, the last year for which a statistical breakdown was available. This middle ground in wine production helps separate the little guys, craft winemakers like Gary and Rosie, from the big producers such as Gallo. The mega producers who produce more than 250,000 cases annually constitute only 4 percent of the wineries in the United States. That's 104 wineries. To confuse matters further, in the last thirty years or so even Gallo, once associated with inexpensive jug wines, has entered the market with quality wines that compete with small quality craft wine makers.

But what is clear is that the 72 percent of the wineries that are independent small producers are dedicated to making craft wines because of their relatively small production.

The figures, however, are misleading in one important way: While the small craft wineries make up the vast majority of wineries, they account for only a small percentage of the wine produced: Gallo alone bottles 30 percent of the wine in the United States, making it the largest national producer. (Constellation remains the largest international producer.) Indeed, while craft wineries, using the 25,000-case production cutoff, may account for 72 percent of the wineries in the United States, they accounted for only 2 percent of the volume of wine produced in 2004.

This helps to explain why small, local wineries outside California often go unnoticed by the American wine-drinking public. When you walk into a wine retailer, you may see a small section dedicated to local wines. Otherwise, what greets you is a sea of wines made by the large producers such as Gallo, Taylor (owned by Constellation), and Paul Masson (owned by the Wine Group, the third largest wine producer in the world). Next priority for commanding shelf space are the other California wines, the French, Italians, Spanish, Germans, and Australians. Then there are the relative newcomers such as the Chilean, South African, and New Zealand wines. To complicate matters further, many of the smaller brand names—which, by their number, give an impression of variety in the market—are owned by conglomerates such as Constellation. One could easily draw the conclusion from their relative absence on the retail shelves that locally owned craft wines not from California hardly exist.

What makes the craft winery phenomenon so remarkable is its sudden growth since 1995 in states other than California. For example, between 1995 and 2007 the number of wineries in Illinois increased from 11 to 83. Similarly in Iowa the number grew from 10 to 62. Oregon saw an increase from 113 to 295, while the number in Missouri rose from 37 to 86, those in Pennsylvania from 52 to 115, and in Wisconsin from 13 to 41. Meanwhile, in the state of Washington the number of wineries increased from 95 to a staggering 451 during that period, making it the state with the second largest number of wineries in the country after California. In the space of one two-year period a winery was opening up at an average of about every two weeks in Washington state.

Compared to other forms of agriculture the winery business is "low risk, low return," said Nelson. Starting a small winery can prove attractive to family-owned farms because of the low start-up costs when compared to the high costs associated with large-scale industrial farming. In many ways winery owners end up having greater control over what they produce than they would in other farming sectors. For one thing, they are not dependent on futures markets. Nor are prices fixed by the government as in the case of milk. To be sure, there are problems. Fungicides, fertilizers, and machinery can be expensive for wineries, too. There can be problems with oversupply and poor weather. And generally it's five years before a newly planted vineyard bears a full crop. But by comparison it's cheaper to run a winery than it is to plant soybeans or corn, or to run a dairy operation.

One consequence is that few wineries fail.

"Almost all wineries have good survival rates—10 percent or less over ten years go bust. Some get sold," Nelson said.

If the risk of failure is relatively low in contrast, say, to the restaurant business, which has an 80 percent failure rate, there is another reality, given the relatively low risk, low return: "You don't really get rich in these small wineries," Nelson said.

Aside from the attraction of low risk, there are other factors, too, for why people start wineries.

"There's a huge heritage. You become part of that heritage, one that goes back thousands of years," Nelson said. "In a world where people have no idea how things are made, they can understand wine. Wine has personality, individuality, diversity. It's the great exception to uniformity."

The great exception?

"*The* great exception," he insisted.

The growth of craft wineries in New York State has mirrored the experience of the rest of the country: In 1995 there were 125 wineries in the state, which long has had a strong winemaking tradition. In 2009 there were 267, according to data from the New York Wine and Grape Foundation.

As winter slowly recedes in March, Gary continues to stir the lees in the barrels, and to smell for off odors. He also tops off the barrels to keep air from getting to the wine. Even if the wine is aging well, it can't be left to age on its own. Gary has a routine of testing for acidity and pH levels. Too much acidity and the wine is said to taste brittle. Too high a pH and it is characterized as flabby.

After their making in the fall, whites are generally aged through the spring before their release. Besides Chardonnay, Gary also makes whites from Vidal Blanc, Pinot Gris, and Riesling. Gary buys Vidal Blanc grapes, a French hybrid, from the Lake Erie region at the western end of the state. They are plentiful and reasonably priced, and for those reasons he sees little reason to plant them. Until his own Riesling and Pinot Gris grapes were ready, he also bought those from the Lake Erie region as well.

While most Chardonnay is aged in barrels, some is also aged in stainless steel to later blend with the oak-aged so that a balance between fruit and crispness can be maintained. The Vidal Blanc, Riesling, and Pinot Gris are aged only in stainless steel. All the whites are aged from three to six months before bottling, whereas the reds must be aged at least a year, depending on the varietal. There is such a thing as aging a wine too long, depending on the varietal, when acidity begins to assert itself and dominate the wine. The result is that it loses its complex of aromas or bouquet.

There is another reason why whites are aged only through the spring: marketing logistics. By that time of year many wineries have run out of whites and release the newest vintage even though the whites could benefit from more aging. The wines continue to improve in the bottle—what is called bottle aging—and Gary says that whites can benefit from aging another eighteen months although he guesses few wine drinkers do so.

Gary's Cabernet Franc, the one red varietal he grows, is also aged in oak. It tends to be bottled at the end of the summer if it is the most recent vintage because Gary will need the barrels for the upcoming vintage. If Gary has the luxury of doing so, Cabernet Franc benefits from aging longer in the barrels. It comes back to an ongoing problem he's had to confront: "You never feel you have enough capacity. You're always juggling—barrels, equipment, space."

Once bottled, reds continue to improve with bottle aging as well.

Late winter is also a time to be vigilant about the potential monsters within the wine. Wine is a living creature, which if nurtured returns the favor. But if ignored, it can become a disaster. That's because wine is transient in nature. In a sense, nature never intended the end result of the fermentation of grape juice to be wine. Instead, the conversion of sugars into alcohol is only an intermediate step. Left untouched by the hand of man and exposed to air, wine will convert to vinegar. Gary's ambition, then, has been to capture something of that fleeting, transient moment. Thus the vigilance, always the testing.

In a good year, the problem may be no more than a malolactic fermentation stalled in the Chardonnay "But that's not unusual for Chardonnay," Gary said.

Malolactic fermentation is a secondary fermentation often done to wines after the initial fermentation at harvest that turned the sugars in the wine to alcohol. Malolactic fermentation converts malic acid, the kind of acid you find in apples, into lactic acid, the kind you find in yogurt. The process helps, along with aging, to soften the wine. This also explains why wines that undergo "ML," as the process is called, are often said to have a slight hint of butter.

One year a monster did rise from the deep in the form of carbon dioxide, which is the fizziness found in soda and Champagne. It happened to the Moon Puppy. It's Gary's sweet wine. And it pays the bills because most wine drinkers are sweet wine drinkers, which can be discouraging to a dry wine person like Gary. Initially, he made it from an under-ripe crop of Cabernet Franc. Sugar is added to sweeten it, and in the more rarefied air of some oeno circles (not so politely described to me as "wine snobs"), it is not considered oeno-correct. But many wineries in the Finger Lakes have such sweet red wines because that's what sells.

Gary recounted the events while tending his wines in the light of a late winter afternoon. He got his first hint of the problem during July when the tasting counter help brought it to his attention.

"When she poured it for me, it was a little fizzy," Gary said.

He picked it up, raised it to his mouth, drank, and could feel the slight effervescence prickle his taste buds.

"Hey, Rosie. The Moon Puppy's turning into Champagne."

"Why do you think that is?"

"Secondary fermentation."

Secondary fermentation is not uncommon and sparkling wine (of which Champagne is the preeminent example) may well have been the result of such an accident. At least that's what the late Dr. Konstantin Frank, a visionary enologist from the Finger Lakes, suggested when his son sought to introduce sparkling wine as another offering at the family's winery. As the story goes, the father responded to his son's proposal with, "They only make sparkling wine in Champagne because they can't get their grapes ripe enough to make decent table wine." That didn't stop his son, however, from making sparkling wine using the Champagne method. Gary figured the problem with his sparkling Moon Puppy was a dirty bottle. The bottles come sterilized from the manufacturer, but sometimes it happens that they have some dirt or dust containing ambient yeast that could cause a secondary fermentation.

Then early in December a bottle of Moon Puppy turned up and the cork had pushed out from the pressure of secondary fermentation. It had emerged about a quarter inch, and the top of the decorative plastic capsule, instead of being flat, was rounded, like the head of a mushroom. Just before Christmas several more bottles did the same— like the dead coming to life.

Gary still suspected unclean bottles. He directed the staff to only sell bottles with a flat top. Any others were poured down the drain.

Because Long Point closes in January, Gary didn't see any more bulging corks while he spent his time testing the new wines in the barrels. But in February, when he reopened and wine sales started picking up, he began finding more problem bottles.

"Just put them aside," he told Rosie and the staff.

On a Saturday in late February a customer came in and said he wanted to buy a case of Moon Puppy for a party. Gary went back into the winery warehouse to personally retrieve a case because he wanted to make sure none of the bottles had protruding corks. He turned the first case right side up (cases are stored upside down so the corks stay moist) and sliced open the sealing tape with a box cutter. When he lifted up the cardboard flaps he had a sickening feeling: three of the bottles out of the twelve-bottle case had protruding corks. He pushed the box aside. He pulled out another box, turned it right side up, and sliced it open. Two bottles had protruding corks.

He opened seven cases. All had the problem.

"What the heck is going on here?" he asked, and he realized it was a bigger problem than just one or two dirty bottles: A monster had gotten loose in his wine.

"Where's that case, Gary?" Rosie called out from the tasting room door.

"I'm coming," he said, as he pulled out the offending bottles from one case and replaced them with bottles with flat tops.

He sold the good case to the customer and hoped that those bottles would taste the way Moon Puppy should. The customer never complained. But Gary worried. "It was like playing Russian roulette." The customer bought the wine for a party. What if one of the bottles exploded?

And Gary kept asking: "What could have gone wrong?"

He pulled the records on the wine's production but couldn't figure it out.

The problem got worse. During the winter Gary keeps the heat down in the winery at fifty-five degrees. It helps age the new wine and saves on the heating bill. As spring warmed, the winery warmed up and with it more bottles were discovered with the mushroom heads: They were fermenting. One day Gary picked up one of the bottles, opened the door to outside from his lab, peeled off the decorative plastic cap, and watched as the pressure in the bottle eased the cork out slowly. Suddenly it popped as if it were a Champagne cork.

"I swear it shot twenty feet into the air."

He was getting occasional complaints from liquor stores. Customers brought the problem bottles back to exchange them. The strange part was that there were bottles of Moon Puppy that appeared not to have undergone the secondary fermentation. They were fine.

Gary suspected that the filter had failed during bottling. Moon Puppy was filtered to remove yeast and to avoid just such a possibility as a secondary fermentation. Filtering was necessary because of Moon Puppy's high sugar content, which feeds the yeast. Moon Puppy has 3.5 percent residual sugar, sweet by any standard.

Maybe the filter had a hole in it? Gary wondered. At one point during bottling it had become clogged so Gary removed it and rinsed it out. He should have installed a new filter. But they cost $400 each. Perhaps he accidentally punctured it? Perhaps he didn't reseat it properly during reinstallation?

One day in May he saw an ominous sign. A small trickle of red wine dribbled out from under the pallets on which he had stacked the Moon Puppy cases. He shifted boxes aside until he found the one with the telltale wet, red wine stain. He turned it upside down, cut open the bulging, wet cardboard, and confirmed what he all but knew: The cork had popped.

The first thing he did was move the cases of Moon Puppy as far away as he could from the propane heater. But he knew the problem wasn't going to stop.

Another day a telltale trickle was found, again. The strange part was that when he found the box the stain was on top, not on the bottom. In other words, because the bottles are stored upside down, the stain was where the bottom of a bottle would be. This time he didn't bother to turn the box right side up. He sliced the sealing tape on the bottom and lifted the flaps. He confirmed his suspicion: A bottle had burst, blowing off the bottom.

"I don't get it, Joe. Where did we go wrong?"

"I don't know," Joe said, equally mystified, because he had helped bottle Moon Puppy the previous summer.

Now it was late spring and there had been about fifteen complaints. Customers told Gary and Rosie that corks were exploding, shooting twenty feet into the living room. He knew he was going to have to pull Moon Puppy from the market.

"I actually dumped maybe fifteen cases down the sink in the lab. I had to do something with the wine. If I had a staff member who opened a case and a bottle exploded, they could lose an eye."

Gary reviewed the records a second time.

"I was flipping through the records and asking, what happened that day? What did I bottle that day?"

As he looked at his log he saw that he bottled the Moon Puppy after another red.

That's when he made the connection: He had only considered bottling the Moon Puppy in isolation but not what had preceded. As he mentally walked through the process, he realized, "Wait a minute. The spouts."

He had bottled two different reds before the Moon Puppy, but they were not sterile filtered. That meant the filling spouts or nozzles in the bottle-filling chamber still contained yeast from the previous reds he had bottled. The spouts were not sterilized once he completed pumping the earlier reds. With those wines, they had no residual sugar for the yeast to feed on, and by that point the yeast had become dormant and gone into a kind of suspended animation. Nonetheless, yeast was still alive. Because sugar is added to Moon Puppy to make it a sweet wine, that provided a new food source for the yeast which lingered in the nozzle heads. At first, they fed slowly because of their dormant state. This explains why only an occasional bottle turned up in late November and December. But after a few months and after the yeast had regained strength, the growth became explosive.

Gary and Joe drove around to liquor stores reclaiming cases of unsold Moon Puppy. They said they were replacing it with the newest vintage.

After picking up the stock at one Cortland liquor store, Gary took it out to his truck. It was a warm spring day. He opened a box, found one of the bottles with the bulging cork, unwrapped the plastic capsule, and watched as the cork eased slowly out under its own power from the pressure in the bottle. It popped.

Because Moon Puppy was his biggest seller, Gary couldn't afford to lose the entire vintage. Now that he knew what the problem was, he would try to reprocess the wine. When someone suggested he sell it as sparkling wine, he dismissed the idea because the bottles couldn't withstand the pressure. "Also, there's the matter of brand integrity. When consumers buy a brand they have certain expectations about what it will taste like. I couldn't have an effervescent Moon Puppy one year and none the next.... Your reputation's on the line."

He feared that at parties someone might say, "Oooh! What's that?"

"Moon Puppy."

"I would never serve that."

On a Saturday late in the spring, Gary and Joe sat on folding chairs in the winery popping corks and pouring Moon Puppy into a sixty-six-gallon sterilized bin. Often, all they had to do was unpeel the plastic cap and once they started to withdraw the cork it would suddenly pop. They wore safety glasses. Throughout the winery you could hear the pop...pop...pop. It was like a New Year's Eve celebration. But no one was celebrating.

"I don't even like Moon Puppy," Gary said, as he told me the story. It was dark outside now—a night sky of late winter with Venus beckoning from the west.

But even though he doesn't care for Moon Puppy, Rosie's retort would ring in his mind: It's our biggest seller. That, he can't deny.

More broken bottles turned up with bottoms blown off.

Pop.

"Did you see that one?"

They popped more than four hundred bottles of Moon Puppy, and Gary pumped the wine into one of the stainless steel tanks.

They recycled about thirty-five cases. Gary lost about twenty-five cases either because the contents of the bottles were dumped, customers returned them to liquor stores, or the bottles burst. At $100 a case with the standard discount, that came out to about $2,500. New bottles, corks, and related expenses pushed the total loss to about $5,000.

The reprocessing wasn't difficult. The carbon dioxide effervesced on its own the same way soda pop goes flat when exposed to air. But Gary had to add sugar because Moon Puppy is intended to be a sweet wine. The fermentation in the bottle converted the sugar to alcohol and the residual sugar had dropped from 3½ percent to 2 percent. There was a corresponding increase in alcohol because of the conversion by yeast.

"I never did figure out how much higher the alcohol was. I was so distraught at that point I didn't want to take any more time with the wine. I would have to guess it was up one to 1½ percent. The wine was probably thirteen to 13½ percent alcohol."

It was a rare vintage indeed.

When he rebottled he made sure that all the hoses and lines in the filling chamber and nozzle heads were sterilized.

In the end, it was part of the learning curve. That's how it had been since he opened the winery: a learning curve. But his consolation was that he knew he was not the only one who had the problem. "I had a lady come in the other day who told me she bought a bottle of white wine from another winery and it blew up in her fridge—misery likes company."

There were, however, two insults to add to the injury. First, because the Moon Puppy bottles were special purchase, they were expensive: $1.35 a piece for a crimson bottle at the time compared to 65¢ for a standard green glass bottle. And now bottles were going to recycling because it wasn't worth the time and effort to wash and sterilize each one.

The second insult came when, after he had withdrawn the effervescent Moon Puppy, a customer came in and asked to buy some more.

"I love the fizzy. It's better than Champagne."

"Customers still ask for it," Gary said.

When they do, he smiles politely. Little do they know, he says, that he's gritting his teeth.

The vineyard in early March is a time of slow stirrings. The vineyard manager has been pruning, but a day promising spring can quickly turn into a snow squall. If severe enough, the vineyardist will retreat to the winery to help Gary. When the storm subsides he returns to the vines.

Bundled up in Carhartt insulated coveralls the color of dirt, Dan Stevens took out his pruning clippers and started pruning.

"At this point I do it automatically, without thinking," he said.

He cut one of last year's fruiting canes and pulled it from the tangle of vines. A couple of inches of snow lay on the ground. Vapor rose from Dan's mouth as he spoke. Dan is a big, robust guy with short, dark hair and a wide jaw. Despite his size, his voice is quiet, even boyish.

When he smiles he strikes you as a big kid unaware of his own strength. Dan started at Long Point in 2006. Joe had moved over to King Ferry Winery to do wholesale and distribution with his wife Kim. Gary enticed Dan away from Sheldrake Point Vineyard on the other side of Cayuga Lake, where he had been the assistant vineyard manager. Dan was only twenty-four at the time, and recently graduated from the state college in Cortland with a degree in political science. His wife, Lindsay, was the assistant winemaker at Sheldrake. Dan, not sure what to do after he graduated, followed his wife's lead. She had recently finished a degree in food science at Cornell. When she took the job at Sheldrake, Dan followed in the vineyard. Today, she's the winemaker at King Ferry Winery, which makes wine under the Treleaven label.

In many ways, Dan is typical of those who come to work at Long Point in that he has a sense of adventure. Some like it and stay, learning on the job. Others stay for a while and then move on. During the early years there was Margaret. She had graduated from nearby Wells College. Rosie and Gary trained her in tasting, and she manned the tasting counter. She stayed for a year. Then there was Jason, with his wife and one-year-old. They were refugees from Boston's urban sprawl. He had worked as a computer programmer, but he and his wife decided to come back to Central New York to raise their child. For the time being he decided to eschew computer code for starting at the bottom in a winery. Eventually he, too, moved on. And there was Shawna, who not only did tastings but promotion as well.

Some simply want to start their lives over. "It's amazing," Gary said about the prospective employees who come looking for work. "I've had lawyers. I've had doctors. They just want to do something different." And the implication is clear. Wine has a kind of allure among those who want to drop out from the establishment, whether it's computer programming, the interminable page-thumbing of case law, or doing rectal exams. Even I was tempted at times. What does it offer? At the least, an honest day's hard labor.

In more recent years, the staff has stabilized. Russ Nalley came to Long Point Winery in 2006 to serve as the marketing manager and conduct tastings. Linda Ehrhart came the same year and is a mainstay at the tasting counter. Myles Mangan is a college student who has been assisting in recent summers at the tasting counter.

Gary recalls a former employee who conducted tastings, Staci Nugent. She did leave but she went on to earn a master's degree in winemaking at the University of California, Davis. The university has one of the most distinguished programs of its kind in the world. Now the former employee is a winemaker in her own right at Keuka Lake Vineyards on the far side of the Finger Lakes.

Dan pruned another cane, pulling it from the vine and casting it aside in the alley between vine rows. In the distance Cayuga Lake glistened from a clear sun whose light bounced off the snow-covered fields on the other side of the lake, making the late winter day sparkle.

Pruning is often used informally to describe the removal of any vegetative matter—canes, shoots, leaves. But technically there are three different phases. *Pruning* itself refers to the winter and spring removal of excess canes. *Shoot thinning* refers to the removal of new shoots later in the season. *Canopy management* is a more general term that refers to trimming excessively vigorous and unwanted shoots and removing leaves. What they all have in common is removing vegetation throughout the season as the vineyard manager attempts to squeeze the best performance from the vines.

When Dan prunes in late winter and early spring, he seeks out two of last year's shoots that have now become new fruiting canes. This means assessing at a glance the shape of the previous year's vine. Two stubs emerge from the main trunk of the vine. From each stub last year's canes spread to left and right. From them the fingers of new canes reach out. The result is that a grapevine looks like a growing candelabra because of the way they've been trained. Which canes are cut depends on the judgment of the pruner. One of the new canes on each side of the trunk is saved, and the remainder of the new canes that were shoots last year are then pruned. The two lone remaining canes on each side of the vine will serve as the upcoming year's fruiting canes from which new shoots—and clusters of grapes—will grow. The idea is to limit the vine system so that nutrients are concentrated in the fruiting canes and new shoots.

Dan clipped through a previous year's fruiting cane. He pulled the old cane from the tangle of vines and pitched it aside in the alley for later pick up. He took the new fruiting cane, light brown and smooth barked, and stretched it to the top wire of the trellis and clipped off the end. That's how he measured the length of the fruiting cane he needed. Now he wove it around the wire located about two and a half feet off the ground in what he calls the "renewal" zone. From here the new shoots will sprout. By the end of the season, those shoots that remain after subsequent shoot thinning will have grown into full-fledged canes. The following year the same selection process will take place, with the new cane—often although not always the closest to the trunk—serving as the new fruiting cane.

"How you prune this year not only determines what your crop for this year will look like but also your crop next year. You have to think in advance," Dan said.

He did the other trunk of the vine to the right now. With new fruiting canes on either side, the candelabra pattern was repeated, if streamlined.

Every year pruning begins earlier and earlier in the season. When Joe first started he had to prune only the one and a half acres of Chardonnay. He could start in late March. But as the Cabernet Franc matured he started pruning in early March. Now that the nearly five acres of Pinot Gris and Riesling are bearing their first crops, Dan has had to push pruning back into February. He predicts that once the vines are fully mature he will start pruning in late January—if pummeling snow storms don't drive him into the winery.

One day as the seasons teetered between a winter chill and a spring warmth, depending on the passing clouds overhead, Gary flushed out his transfer hoses and wine pump and recounted the story of how he got into winemaking.

It started in 1976. He was twenty-four and needed a place to live. He had just graduated from college with a dual major in economics and political science. He had returned to Syracuse but didn't know what he wanted to do. Politics perhaps? He always had some ambition in that direction.

But at the moment he needed a place to live.

Only the story gets more complicated, he said. "Because my grandfather made wine."

Lodged beneath the veneer of a recently educated young man fresh out of college who thought he had the answers to life was a memory from childhood of the old man—short, balding, with a moonlike face—who would disappear at the door to his cellar, his bald pate descending as he walked down the steps to be swallowed up by the earth. As a young boy Gary watched his grandfather—from whom he would inherit his lack of hair, among other things—descend into a dark, unknown world to which he, Gary, was not permitted.

Then, magically, Grandpa Dom reappeared at the door with a glass pitcher of red wine in one hand—what the WASPs who have no passion for life derisively snub as "dago red." When he appeared, the kitchen filled with the delicious perfume of red wine, delicious enough that you could almost taste the grape clusters fermenting on the vine. Sometimes, as was often the case with Italian-American families, his grandfather poured Gary a little wine in a small glass. It wasn't one of the fancy, high-stemmed wine glasses that a sophisticate drinks from. Instead, it was just a small, simple *paisano* glass, the kind to sip gingerly from under the shade of a lemon tree outside a taverna on a barren, sun-washed hillside overlooking the azure Adriatic.

It was a consecration when his grandfather gave him a glass. The fragrance was redolent of everything good and wonderful about the old man.

His grandfather laughed uproariously when Gary made a sour face at the taste of the wine. He could never finish the glass.

"That's not all," Gary said.

There was the memory of the times when his grandfather and his cronies, other stoop-shouldered, old Italian men, would head down to the cellar to do a man's work. His grandfather's head disappeared into the earth, followed by the heads of his compatriots, Italian-American grandfathers who were now reaping the harvest of their later years and doing what they really wanted to do: make wine. Soon you could feel the whole house creak.

"What's that, grandma?" Gary asked.

"Dominic is pressing grapes," she said, pronouncing the name the Italian way with the emphasis on the long O—"*Do*-minic."

The house shuddered, as the old men pressed, unseen, in the cellar on the north side of Syracuse. His grandfather built the press so a house beam supporting the first floor acted as a pressure point to squeeze the grapes.

Gary listened as the house creaked. His grandmother crossed herself, then looked up to see if heaven would come crashing down in her face while glass jars vibrated across the white enamel surface of a kitchen table until one teetered at the edge. It toppled over and smashed on the floor before she could catch it.

"You're wrecking my kitchen," she screamed furiously in Italian down the cellar entrance, into this region where only men were permitted to tread. You could hear laughter from the cellar.

Gary giggled. And his grandmother smiled silently.

One day some years later, Gary's grandfather, who by then was eighty-five years old, climbed slowly down the stairs, as he had so many times before, to fill his pitcher with red wine. He lost his balance and fell. His head struck something hard as he tumbled down the stairs and he died.

His grandfather and grandmother had long been dead when Gary graduated from college and needed a place to live. His father told him that Grandpa Dom's house was for rent, cheap. "By the way, the wine press is still in the basement," he said.

The wine press? Gary was intrigued.

Gary finished flushing out the transfer hoses and wine pump and was taking a break from his story as he poured a glass of red.

"You gotta try this. This has body. And good fruit."

It did, and provided a welcome warmth from the 55-degree chill of the winery and the dregs of winter outside.

He continued his story: When he went to see his grandparents' house, it was in the empty kitchen, long bare of his grandmother's touch, that the feeling started to come back of that redolent past— the family dinners, his grandma fussing over him because he was her favorite. But then she told all her grandchildren that. Then he remembered the house shuddering and the glass crashing.

He looked at the door to the cellar and into a world long denied him, and remembered his grandfather emerging from the cellar. Gary walked over to the door, opened it, and flipped the light switch. He walked slowly down the steps.

He found the wine press in the middle of the concrete floor just as his grandfather had left it, the house jack used to press the wine still positioned under the support beam.

So that was it. That was the secret to the mysterious ways of men to which little boys were not privy. The basement had low rafters. Gary is five feet nine inches tall, and still he had to stoop. But his grandfather was so short, he had no difficulty standing up—"He could have jump-roped down there, he was so short."

Gary stared at the press. His grandfather had constructed it out of tongue-and-groove oak flooring. The press was as round as an oak barrel except that it wasn't bowed in the middle and there were quarter-inch gaps between the staves. When his grandfather pressed the grapes the juice squeezed out at the bottom through the gaps. The basic principle is still used today, and the reason you press grapes at all is because if you didn't a lot of grape juice would remain behind in the dregs.

Gary still has the wood cage to the press. It languishes in a corner of his garage, a gray-brown cage dark from years of pressings and, now, years of disuse. Indeed, it is constructed of tongue-and-groove oak floorboards; his grandfather didn't bother removing the tongues and grooves, thinking the way practical men do: if it works, it works.

Even though, as Gary remembered, the light in the cellar was dim— the small windows, unwashed for years, only permitted a gray twilight to enter—he could see that the old press appeared to be in operating order. It was effective and yet simple. The pressure was exerted by a conventional post jack. You placed a round board inside the pressing cage atop the grapes and the jack atop the press board. With the jack under the house beam, you turned the screw of the jack with a wrench.

"I like this," Gary recalled thinking to himself as he stared at the press. "I like this a whole lot."

Jack, Gary's older brother, said he wasn't surprised at Gary's reaction. "He always was the maverick in the family." There are some stories Jack won't tell about his little brother, the wisecracking, in-your-face kid from Syracuse's northside. But his little brother always did have an appetite for trying new things—making air-cured dry Italian salami and prosciutto, for instance. He had turned down athletic scholarships to nearby colleges to go to one in Oklahoma just because he wanted to get away from Syracuse. And before he settled down he tried just about any job that came his way: construction, flipping hamburgers, working in a car wash, bartending. Perhaps the most unusual was "scraping pigeon shit off the steeples at Syracuse University," Gary volunteered in such a way that you would think he was proud.

In the cellar to the old house, Gary's grandfather had built a circular form and poured a concrete base that stood about eighteen inches high. On to the freshly poured concrete he had placed a car tire and pressed it down to make a circular channel. The idea was that the wine flowed into the channel. "It was ingenious, when you looked at it. You could still see the tire imprint." Then, on one side of the concrete base his grandfather scooped out a notch and stuck a piece of folded tin into the still wet concrete to make a spout. From the spout the juice would pour into buckets that would then go to the aging barrel.

Gary rented the house for $150 a month. And now he had a mission while he flipped hamburgers and scraped pigeon droppings from steeples.

That first year his father and Jack helped him make wine. Gary bought his first used whiskey barrel. They pried off the top two iron rings that held the staves together, pried out the lid and tried scraping out as much of the interior surface as they could to remove the saturated fragrance of corn mash whisky.

Did it affect the taste?

"Did it! That was some pretty rough stuff," Gary said.

The result was wine that had the distinctive bouquet of corn mash. No matter how much they scraped the insides of the barrels and scoured them out at the local car wash. Not that you couldn't drink it. It was just, well, different.

The next year they made wine, again. Then Gary's father died at age fifty-eight, keeling over from working three jobs, and Gary was on his own.

In the years since, Gary married and divorced, and he became a nuclear medicine technologist. Eventually the family sold his grandfather's house and Gary moved on. But he took the oak cage of the press with him. It was a tie to his past.

When he left his grandfather's house he found friends who were willing to make wine with him and let him press grapes in their basements or garages. But when it was no longer fun they would politely ask him to find another place to make his wine.

The problem was Gary took winemaking too seriously. For his buddies, making wine was supposed to be fun. And drinking wine while you made it was even better. And it was even better when the garlic pizzas with hot peppers arrived to accompany the winemaking. They were fun times. Up to a point. Because after a day's work and everybody went home, Gary always kept calling, nagging. "Did you do this? Did you do that?" he recalled. One time he called to find out how the wine was doing and discovered that it was on top of an agitating washing machine.

"What are you doing? You could kill the fermentation," Gary said. Making wine was a serious business for Gary, like taking care of a newborn. He fussed over it endlessly.

Sooner or later he would be asked to leave. So, as an amateur winemaker he lived an itinerant life around Syracuse, depending on the kindness of others as he learned his art. Then, one by one, he began to get awards for his wines, so that by the time he opened Long Point he had won more than sixty awards in amateur winemaking competitions. Today they sit in a case on the wall of the addition he built to the garage where he made his wine after he married Rosie. The case is stuffed. There are so many awards that they present a jungle of red, blue, and white ribbons and bronze, silver, and gold medals.

That was his apprenticeship. Twenty-four years. When he opened Long Point, his life embodied the old maxim, no wine before its time. And because of the fruit of the vine he was saved from the seductions of a career in politics.

SPRING

SPRING ARRIVES, although not necessarily to the equinox, because the Finger Lakes have their own seasonal rhythm, defying the wishful thinking of the calendar. Rather, the warming *feel* of spring doesn't arrive until April—sometimes not even until mid-April—when the sun finally begins to emerge with some constancy, providing an antidote to the long Upstate winters. Finally, winter's warm longings are realized, and the snowbirds start returning from Florida and Arizona.

In the vineyard, the vines respond to spring, too, and the true measure of spring's arrival is that the buds start breaking. There is a visceral sense of the vines coming to life.

"Here's one that's almost ready to pop," Dan said. He fingered a bud on a shoot that was about a quarter inch long and not quite as wide. It had the "fuzzy"—the soft, gray fuzzy surface that can mean death to the bud if it appears too soon in winter.

Over the last few weeks the buds had swelled from the rising temperatures. Dan examined another vine where most of the buds had popped. The fuzzy membrane of the bud had split open and shoots were pushing out with miniature tendrils, green leaves just emerging from the shell.

The signs of change had been on the vines for the last few weeks. You could see it in the pruning scars that bled with water.

It's also time for hilling down. A little later Dan made a sweeping pass through the vineyard row atop the old Case tractor Gary had bought secondhand. After months of working under gray winter skies, riding a tractor with the sun on your back was redemption: The whole sky opened up and you felt freed from the chill of winter.

The tractor chattered as the blade of the plow dug into the long ridge of earth underneath the line of trellis wire. The effect was a slowly curling six-inch-high wave of dirt that rolled over and fell away from the base of the vine trunk.

The vines were hilled up in late fall, after the harvest, when the vineyard manager plowed up a ridge of dirt high enough to cover the graft on the vine where the American rootstock joined the European budwood. The rootstock provides resistance to the diseases that thwarted early efforts to grow European grapes when European settlers established colonies on the Atlantic seaboard, and that would continue to frustrate American devotees of European viticulture such as Thomas Jefferson. The budwood provides the European taste that, for better or worse, is the established standard in wine tasting. The problem, however, is that the scar of the graft remains vulnerable to cold in the northeastern winters. So, late in fall, the wineries in the Finger Lakes hill up to insulate the graft union from the cold. The deep snows add another layer of insulation.

In spring the insulating earth has to be removed because the scar of the union remains vulnerable, now to the diseases and pests of summer. Soil must also be removed because the union between rootstock and budwood is not entirely agreeable. It's more in the way of a forced marriage. Given their genetic preferences the two different vines would rather be matched with their own kind. If you did not hill down, the European budwood would try to establish its own roots, growing down into the soil and bypassing the American. But then the European would become vulnerable to phylloxera, a deadly little bug that almost destroyed the vineyards of France in the nineteenth century. They were saved only by grafting them onto American rootstock. Moreover, the American rootstock, if not pruned of shoots, can grow into a vine bearing American grapes that rob nutrients from the European budwood.

One mid-April morning I realized that the forest lining the edge of Cayuga Lake had suddenly greened—a young, modest spring green. The sun had been shining for several days, the temperatures had risen into the high 50s and low 60s, and now the maples that dominate the deciduous in this northern latitude had dawned pointillist dabs of pale green that shimmered in the spring breeze.

At the winery, Gary was down on his hands and knees inserting his head into a manway, a twenty-two-inch-round hatch in one of the stainless steel tanks. He began to crawl through it in his rain suit and his yellow-trousered legs disappeared like the tail of a fish slipping into a watery cave. In the stainless steel tunnel he felt the pressure against his aging knees, the kind of pressure that makes it difficult "to ski powder anymore," he complained.

Gary's feet disappeared at one end of the manway and he clambered out of the tunnel at the other and into the ten-foot-high tank with a bucket in hand. He had already removed the lid from the tank. When the 3,000-liter tank is filled with wine, a stainless steel cover, five feet across, is placed on top as if it were a giant lid to a cooking pot, except that it has a round pneumatic rubber gasket that Gary inflates to make an airtight seal. Now the lid was off and the tank open.

Gary's arm swept back and forth across the curved stainless steel wall as he scrubbed it down with a large sponge and a chlorine solution. He resembled a window washer as he worked his way down the walls and across the stainless steel floor. He worked backward into the manhole opening until his yellow legs reemerged outside the tank.

After he rinsed off the chlorine solution with a hot water hose, Gary crawled back into the tank, complained once more about the pressure on his knees, and scrubbed down the interior with a clean sponge and a citric acid solution to neutralize the chlorine. When he finished, he backed out through the manway, his hand sweeping the surface with the sponge as he retreated into the tunnel. Then he rinsed the tank from above to wash out the citric acid.

By the utilitarian looks of it, Long Point Winery could just as easily house an industrial production line. The work area where the wine is processed takes up the rear three-quarters of the building, a large warehouse where the wine ages in the oak barrels, while cases of bonded bottles are stacked to the ceiling. The cavernous fifty-by-seventy-five-foot room is insulated with twelve inches of insulation in the ceiling and nine inches in the walls. A towering 5,000-liter stainless steel tank with a refrigeration jacket around it, as well as 3,000-liter and two 2,000-liter tanks line one wall near the oversized garage door. Sixty-gallon white oak barrels are arranged in neat rows two to a cradle, and the cradles are stacked as many as four high (placed there by a propane-powered Toyota forklift). The smooth, well-scrubbed concrete floor is so clean you could eat off of it. It makes me think of a clean room in a computer-chip manufacturing facility: no dripping, moldy cellars here suitable for those distinctly French creations, mushrooms, cheese, and, yes, wine.

A cozy tasting room in the front quarter of the building has a wide-angle view of Cayuga Lake through a bank of double-hung windows. Offices are located over the tasting room, where Gary and Rosemary sometimes spend the night rather than drive back to Cortland.

Long Point currently produces about 10,000 gallons of wine annually. Someday, Gary would like to make 18,000.

Rosie emerged from her office on to the balcony overlooking the warehouse and called out. You could tell she was flustered.

"I'm missing 168 gallons of wine," she said, her voice echoing between the wine barrels. "I can't find them anywhere. Are you sure you've been recording what you've been taking?"

She's filling out the required monthly audit for the federal Alcohol and Tobacco Tax and Trade Bureau. Gary shrugged his shoulders.

"I can't find them anywhere," she repeated, an edge to her voice.

Another silence, and Rosie walked down the stairs from the balcony to confront Gary.

"Are you sure you've been doing the paperwork?" she asked, arching one eyebrow beneath her dark brunette bob. There's a hint of an accusation. It's a conversation they've had before because Gary dislikes doing the paperwork.

"If we don't find them, I'll have to inventory everything again," Rosie said. She turned in frustration to the stacked, bonded boxes of wine towering above her, containing some ten thousand bottles of wine.

Gary deflected the accusatory hint by saying nothing. His shoulders shrugged. Then, "Have the girls been filling out all the paperwork properly?" he asked, referring to the tasting room help.

"How about the case you gave your brother? Did you record that?" she countered.

He nodded. "That's not 168 gallons."

"I'll go back and go over the receipts again," Rosie said. She turned and headed up the stairs, resigning herself to the prospect of having to do another inventory.

"There is more paperwork to do for a winery than in accounting for nuclear materials in a hospital," Gary said. "You have to account for every ounce of wine you make." As a nuclear medicine technician, he knows. Rosie does the paperwork for the winery and the Feds monitor all aspects of commercial winemaking. It's not because the government is disposed to Prussian efficiency. Nor does it stem from any altruistic concern for public health. It's simply that for the Feds—the U.S. Treasury, specifically—wine translates into revenue.

Gary removed a bung from the top of a barrel and inserted his wine thief to extract some Chardonnay. Today he was tasting to see if the vintage was ready for release. He poured the Chardonnay into a glass, swished it around at nose level, and took his time inhaling. He lifted the glass to his lips and tasted, the glass lingering at his mouth. He nodded.

A silence followed as he thought about it.

"This is good," he said. "This is very good. It's so good I think I'm going to sell it for $35 a bottle."

But he's joking, because the Chardonnay market has deflated by 25 percent in recent years. What Gary might have charged $15.99 for back then is now down to $11.99 a bottle.

"The problem is that Chardonnay has become very abundant. They were over planted," Gary said.

In hindsight, he contributed in his own small way to the problem when he put in his Chardonnay vineyard. Then there was something of a shift in taste from whites to reds because of the reputed health benefits of reds. But Gary thinks he's seeing that abate as wine drinkers are learning to appreciate the qualities of the whites that the Finger Lakes can produce.

Gary passed judgment: The Chardonnay was ready.

"It still has some nice fruit on it, some nice oak."

By fruit, he means that it has aromas suggestive of fresh fruit, although not necessarily of grapes. In the case of Chardonnay, it can be apple, melon, lemon, and pineapple. These aromas will be enhanced by the oak tannins during bottle aging.

Oak complements Chardonnay, if there's not too much. That said, it's a delicate balancing act between maintaining some of the crispness one expects of whites and some body. And it's all to be found in the way the fruit, oak, and lactic acid play off each other.

Chardonnay always occupied an exalted place in Gary's family because it was his Italian grandmother's favorite wine. When he would visit her in the nursing home, she would always ask, "Did you bring me some Chardonnay?"

It's also his mother's favorite wine, and there is the poignant sense of history repeating itself because now that she is in a nursing home, the same nursing home his grandmother was once in, she always asks: "Did you bring me some Chardonnay?"

Gary poured me a tasting. Yes, compared to what I had tasted earlier in winter, it was fuller. You could catch the oak. Ever so slightly I could taste the butter. But the decision to bottle the wine is not as clear as it sounds. Rather, it's more of a slow evolution, as week after week he tasted the maturing wine, until a crucial moment was reached.

"You can tell. It develops more of a roundness. It's more mature. It develops better balance," Gary said. The roundness and maturity result in mouthfeel, filling the palate with hints of other tastes, hints I struggle to understand, but which I can detect when Gary identifies them: In other words, the power of suggestion.

Rosie returned.

"Okay. I went over the paperwork again. It's sixteen gallons," she said, adding quickly, defensively, "I was off by a decimal point." Clearly she's relieved she doesn't have to do another inventory.

"And before it was how much?" Gary asked loudly, well knowing it was 168 gallons. But he's making up for the accusatory hint, the way husbands do, with a barely concealed display of gloating.

She walked down the steps from the balcony.

"168."

"From 168 to 16 is quite a difference."

"I made a mistake in a decimal point."

She walked up to him and leaned her head on his gymnast's shoulder. It was as if to say something more than I'm sorry. It was more in the nature of, honey, why are we in this business? She's lost her usual self-possession and now she's vulnerable.

Gary wrapped his arm around her shoulder and patted her comfortingly, as if he knew the answer to her query.

April is also the time when the wine-tasting season begins in earnest. Although Long Point Winery reopens for business in February, April marks the real advent of the tasting season, because now Upstaters begin to stir and crawl out from under the winter shadows to rediscover a world warmed by sun. There's an almost giddy feeling of redemption, and one response is to head out to the wineries where you can taste sunshine on the palate and absorb a greening world outside the double-hung windows with a lake in the distance.

The wine-tasting season is as important to the winery as healthy buds are to the future of the wine crop because of one imperative: You can make all the wine you want, but you have to sell it, too.

Tasting rooms are the most important means for marketing craft wines at small wineries like Long Point given that few national distributors will distribute wine from wineries that don't have volume and long-established pedigrees. A New York State survey found that 85 percent of the sales from the wineries around Cayuga Lake are from tasting rooms. Special events are one way to get wine lovers and those who might become wine lovers out to the wineries.

For the Barlettas, the start of the season is marked by the Wine and Herb Festival. Most of the wineries along Cayuga Lake participate in the two-weekend event, when enophiles make the rounds of the wineries, picking up a free herb plant, tasting wine, and hopefully, buying. The wineries sponsor similar special events throughout the year to attract customers to the tasting rooms. Long Point participates in a half dozen under the sponsorship of the Cayuga Wine Trail, which is a marketing group of wineries around the Lake.

For its herb giveaway one spring, Long Point was assigned eggplant. Eggplant an herb?

"Don't ask me how we got that one," Rosie said.

But that she could live with. Because she had two other pressing concerns. As she chopped onions on the counter in her Cortland kitchen—thirty pounds of onions for the Italian stew she was making that would be served over the next two days, Saturday and Sunday, the last weekend of April, to potential wine-buying customers—she was concerned because wine sales had been lean for the last few months.

"We need to regain our momentum," she said.

Hopefully, the Wine and Herb Festival would do that.

Then there was the second worry. Her daughter-in-law was due to give birth any day. What if she went into labor during the festival? Rosie, of course, wanted to be there for the birth of her second grandchild.

She didn't get to bed until half past one that night. And no matter how much she washed her hands, the smell of onions always lay on her fingertips.

Gary arrived at the winery at 7:30 on Saturday morning. Rosie was late because she decided to make another small pot of stew just in case they ran out. She arrived at 9:30, just in time to help set up the collapsible tables in the winery for receiving the customers. At one table, by the door, customers would have their festival tickets stamped, indicating that they had made their port-of-call. John Chandler and Jackie Cobey, friends from down the road who wanted to open their own winery some day, had volunteered to process the customers and ladle out stew in small

Styrofoam cups. Joe would offer tastings. Then the customers would head into the tasting room proper where Rosie and Gary would offer more tastings and, they hoped, work the cash register.

At a quarter to ten Rosie and Gary realized the magnitude of what they were confronting. By then the customers were lined up outside the winery. The line stretched across the gravel parking lot. It was a beautiful, cloudless spring morning, crisp, the sun floating majestically in the sky. And now, indeed, enophiles had crawled out from the winter's shadows to eagerly stand in line to take in the truth of wine.

On cue, it seemed, Rosie received a phone call when the doors opened at ten. It was her son Tony. His wife had gone into labor.

"It wasn't urgent, but they are going to drop the dog at my house and head for the hospital," she said.

Rosie looked at the line of wine aficionados outside. She realized then that she would not be there for the birth of her grandson. The winery was about to be overwhelmed and things risked spiraling out of control.

"Love you, Ton. Keep me posted," she said, and hung up.

She was not disappointed when they opened. One could almost hear the cash register go ching … ching … ching, even though it was the kind that clicked ringlessly.

At 11:30 Tony called again.

"He's here."

Mercifully, labor had been short.

Rosie would tell complete strangers, "I'm a grandmother. Nine pounds, thirteen ounces."

She worked the cash register, and, she realized, it was turning out to be one of their best days yet.

"You're the *desert* of the wine trail," one customer told her. At first she thought he was referring to their location on the east side of Cayuga Lake, where, at the time, there were only two wineries along the middle shore.

"No. I mean it's because your wines are so dry," he said.

That was a compliment. It was a vindication because Gary was a dry-wine man in a world of sweet-wine drinkers.

Rosie didn't leave the winery until almost 7:30 that evening. Officially, the winery closes at five. But festival-goers kept showing up.

You couldn't help but get the feeling that some were afraid they would miss out on their free eggplant. Anyway, that's when the stew ran out—Rosie's Italian stew that was supposed to last for two days. That was Rosie's signal to leave.

It's a sin in the small winery business to walk away from potential customers at any time of day. A potential customer is a potential returning customer, attracted by the distinctive qualities of a crafted wine. But while running out of food gave Rosie the excuse to leave the winery, there was the other consequence: Not only would she go to the hospital to see her new grandson but also she would have to go shopping and make more Italian stew for the next day, Sunday. Slicing more onions. More eggplant. Potatoes.

Meanwhile, Gary stayed to improvise. In the refrigerator, he found flour tortilla shells and made eggplant and cheese tortillas. After Gary closed, he would have to do the cleanup by himself. The restrooms needed to be cleaned. Empty bottles needed to be recycled, the tasting room resupplied with wine, and record keeping updated. Then the terrazzo floor in the tasting room had to be mopped.

As Rosie drove home, she knew it was a good day at the winery. She remembered the official opening of the season the first time they participated in the Wine and Herb Festival. That was the spring of 2000, their first year. They had only one wine to offer, the Ciera, made from Grenache and Vidal Blanc grapes. In some ways the day was a disaster. "I forgot to bring the money for the cash register," she said. "For that matter, I didn't even know how to work a cash register—I kept entering the numbers wrong." She knew how to operate the most sophisticated of digital X-ray machines, but she didn't know how to operate a cash register, and it would be a nightmare later to disentangle for bookkeeping. But the day was also a success. "We sold every bottle of Ciera. At ten o'clock that night we were putting new labels on more bottles for the next day." This was back in the days when they still labeled by hand.

"This year we had a dozen wines to offer and the line of customers stretched out the door," she said.

After she visited her grandson at the hospital, the other reality awaited: shopping for more ingredients for Italian stew. She didn't get to Tops until 10 p.m. and she was just about the only customer in the store. On a typical Saturday evening in the Upstate town of Cortland, residents are more likely to be out bowling at one of the town's two bowling alleys, or at the movies at the town's one cinema, or watching TV at home after a day of golf at one of the town's four golf courses. If they're college students attending the local state college they might be drinking themselves silly in the bars on Main Street because the semester was coming to an end.

Rosie pushed the cart down the vegetable aisle of the supermarket under the bright fluorescent lights. She bought more eggplant, and 24 thirty-two-ounce cans of diced tomatoes, 2 twenty-pound bags of potatoes, and, yes, another ten-pound bag of onions. In the meat section she picked up more packages of sweet Italian sausage.

When Rosie got home she found Samantha, the golden retriever, crawled into bed with Gary. Rosie wasn't going to argue. She lay down on the sofa and fell asleep the moment she closed her eyes.

Somehow, Rosie awoke when the alarm went off at five in the morning. She forced herself to open her eyes and sit up, resisting the desire to sleep more, because she knew if she didn't get up, she wouldn't— not for a long, long time.

She began chopping in the kitchen. Onions, eggplant, potatoes. In the early morning there was just a suggestion of thin gray on the horizon. Samantha showed up outside the kitchen door in the dining room, circling three times before lying down with a snort and a "glmph!", not understanding this change in morning routine. Rosie finished chopping the vegetables, opened the oven door, and pushed the pan of vegetables in to bake. "That's the secret to Italian stew. Bake the vegetables first," Rosie said.

That day wine sales exceeded those of Saturday. Rosie stayed in touch with Tony by phone. The baby was fine and that's what mattered. The cash register clicked quietly. And somehow Rosie made it through the day, but not before Gary told her, "You look awful. You should see the dark rings around your eyes." She knew he was just concerned, but sometimes the lug lacked in the social-skills department.

When she pulled up at the house that evening she dreaded only one thing: the kitchen. She had left dirty pots, pans, and scraps of food everywhere, potato skins, eggplant slices, spilled tomato sauce. A dirty stirring spoon had fallen and spattered tomato sauce on the floor. She got out of the car with her dirty stew pots nested in her arms and fumbled with the key to the kitchen door. There was a part of her that just wanted to cast everything into the kitchen chaos and go straight to bed.

After the door swung open to the landing and she climbed the short flight of steps to the kitchen, she stopped and wanted to rub her eyes. Except she couldn't because her hands clutched the dirty stew pots. If she threw the stew pots into the chaos she could rub her eyes. But she couldn't because there was no chaos. All the pots and pans were scrubbed spotless. The floor had been mopped. Everything was put away, and the kitchen was clean and airy.

"I knew you were going to need some help," said a note on the kitchen counter left by Kathi, her best friend. Rosie placed the pots she was carrying into the sink.

"She's my best friend and she's my only friend," Rosie said, in a refrain she had long found comfort in. Kathi. They had raised their kids together after Rosie's divorce and before she met Gary, and Kathi always had a way of coming to the rescue.

Rosie smiled. Little Nick's okay. He had been named after her grandfather Niccolo. And it was the best weekend for wine sales they'd had yet. At that point she headed upstairs to bed. As for the dirty pots in the sink, she thought, let Gary do them.

On an afternoon in May, Rosie recalled how she got mixed up with Gary and winemaking. She sat at her desk in the winery office on the second floor above the tasting room. In addition to the desk, it contained file cabinets and a computer where she managed the business, recording sales and bottle purchases, paying utility bills. But what drew my eye was the picture window. From her aerie one could take in the sweeping view of Cayuga Lake emerging out of the north and trailing off to the south. The trees along the shore were a rich, verdant spring green.

"It goes back to when we were dating," Rosie said. They started dating in 1983. Rosie quickly became aware that Gary had his "wine thing." He loved making wine more than anything else. And that was the source of Rosie's ambivalence about him. Not that she was ambivalent about wine. No, she acknowledged, she's a true daughter of Italy. And that was part of what attracted her to Gary. Her grandfather, Niccolo, being Italian, also made wine in his cellar.

This is when I realized that among certain generations of Italian-American families Italian grandfathers almost always made wine in the cellar. "Yeah, I used to make wine in the cellar," Joe, my Italian barber who arrived in 1953, told me when I sat in his barber's chair one day. "Everyone made wine in the cellar." It was just one more way, along with celebrating the feast days, of maintaining the connection to the patria. True, maybe the wine wasn't always very good. Gary once gave me a taste of some made by a neighbor. "This is *true* Dago red. It's really bad." He insisted I taste it before I tasted one of his Syrahs. It was made from a blend of three or four different grape varieties. It was harsh and bitter compared to the softness of the Syrah, which slaked and soothed the fire left by the homemade red. And there's the story my wife tells me about her Italian grandfather who every year made his wine in the cellar, then got together with his buddies to see who had made the best vintage. "And every year," she said, "they voted his the worst. Every year. The worst. No matter how much he tried. Every year. He died after carrying lugs of grapes home for making wine. And when he died, his best friend asked my grandmother if he could take the wine left in the cellar. He took it, drank it, and ended up in the hospital." Or so the story was told to her.

Movie director Francis Ford Coppola, who has his own winery in California, similarly recalled, in an interview in *Decanter* magazine: "We had wine at the family table ever since I can remember. My grandfather had made wine at home all his life. My parents would water it down, and we didn't really like it.... Wine was certainly connected with memory, of hearing stories about making it in the basement every year, and giving some to the neighbors; generally an association in my mind with happiness, sharing, and family."

So, if you were an Italian-American grandfather, you made wine, whatever the quality. And I suspect that if you ever find someone who says their Italian grandfather didn't make wine in the cellar, either they're lying or it's a case of bad bloodlines. Maybe some Tunisian mixed in from those who crossed over the strait between Carthage and Marsala selling dried dates or waging war. Or maybe a German Crusader who stopped by on his way to the Holy Land and liked what he saw in olive-complexioned beauty but whose DNA could never quite give up quaffing beer.

Rosie recalls that when she was a little girl, her grandfather, a big, tall man with a kindly smile on a very round face, would hand her a water pitcher and direct her softly, "Go down to the barrels." It's a contrast, of course, to Gary's experience, because his grandmother was trying to shelter him from the ways of men. But Rosie served her grandfather, and willingly. In the cellar she would fill up the pitcher with his homemade red and the fragrant bouquet of wine would fill the musty cellar air as she turned the tap. When she returned with the full pitcher, he smiled and gave her a hug. "He always had lots of hugs. He was a quiet man and didn't talk a lot. But he would pick me up, put me on his knee, and tell me how much he loved me. Then he would give me a dime and say, 'Now go to the store and buy some candy.'"

The wine was one of the reasons Rosie loved Gary. His winemaking brought the reassurance of the past back to her.

The *problem* with their shared romance for wine started when she invited Gary to make wine in her cellar. In 1984 Rosie bought a 1920s Dutch colonial painted cornflower blue with a big front porch on a tree-lined street in Cortland, a nice place to raise her two boys now that she was divorced and a single mom. Gary was living in a cabin on a lake a few miles north of Cortland and had no place to make wine. After all, the kindness of friends who offered him their garages and basements had worn thin. Rosie saw it as an opportunity. They had been courting and were pretty serious. But how to get this guy—who was gun-shy about relationships after his first marriage failed—to commit?

"It's got a nice wine cellar," she told him the day she returned from making an offer on the house. Meaning, it had a stone cellar that could be turned into a nice wine cellar. That was the lure.

"It is a nice wine cellar," Gary said the day he saw it. It was stone with a concrete floor, and if you ignored the furnace in the back and the cobwebs in the rafters it could have been a stone cellar in Italy.

Gary, either not being sophisticated in the wiles of women or not caring, took the bait.

One day in early September of that year Rosie awoke at 6 a.m. to see through the bedroom window a big refrigerated produce truck from Syracuse parked in front of her house. Gary had called some friends over to help carry wooden lugs of red grapes from the truck to the cellar window. It was a seemingly endless stream of lugs, which were piled almost to the height of the ceiling in the refrigerated truck.

"Where's Gary?" she asked with a sense of foreboding when she went outside in the early morning air. Another lug went by. Gary was serious.

"In the cellar."

"How much did you order?" she asked when she found him relaying the lugs through a window and stacking them on the cellar floor by the furnace.

"Two hundred." That's lugs, which comes out to about two tons of grapes.

And he grinned, the grin saying: You want wine? You got wine.

Now Rosie understood why Gary's friends evicted him from their garages and basements.

There is a photograph of those days when Gary started making wine at Rosie's, showing a younger, thinner Gary who still had hair, standing in front of wooden lugs stacked two and three deep by the furnace and up to the height of his shoulders. The grin had given way to a triumphant smile.

There's another picture from that time, one of Rosie while they were making wine. She is a slender, pretty young woman with long, brunette waves and you would think that in her youth she had been a flower child of the 1960s: On her face she has a look of dazed innocence.

Her look also reveals how differently Gary and Rosie viewed winemaking. As most couples do, they were talking at cross-purposes, each choosing to believe what he or she wanted to believe. When Rosie was thinking that Gary could make wine in the cellar, she was thinking of a small back cellar room measuring about ten feet by six feet, what had once been a coal bunker.

But Gary had something else in mind: the whole cellar. So he was filling it up with two tons of grapes and oak barrels.

That was the beginning.

Next, Rosie recalled, came the fruit flies. This was a few days later. The fruit flies invaded the house and everyone knew the fruit flies had invaded the house when they could feel them flying up their noses at night as they tried to sleep.

"Ma, there's bugs," Tony cried out in the dark. He was nine at the time. And all night long you could hear hands in the dark swatting ears, noses.

"Ma, there's bugs," Denny echoed a little later.

You could hear swatting in the dark.

Rosie began to wonder if there were limits to this compulsion. She was beginning to lose her innocence.

There's the story about the time the pilot light went out for the hot water heater.

"Hey, Gar," Rosie said one morning, calling him at the hospital. He had the early shift and had left before the others were up. "There's no hot water."

"What do you mean there's no hot water? I took a shower this morning."

"There's no hot water."

"I'll call the heating guy."

When the plumber arrived he went down to the cellar. At the time four oak barrels with the tops removed lined the cellar walls and in them crushed grapes fermented, giving off little bubbly burps. The plumber took in the barrels dubiously. Then he got down on his knees and checked the hot water tank. The pilot light was out. He opened the pilot valve to ignite it. Nothing. The spark sputtered out. He did it again. The flame sputtered and died.

Then he stood up.

He was a big man, Rosie said, the kind of guy who needs a lot of air to fill big lungs, and his head almost hit the floor joists above him—he was six foot three, a good bit taller than Gary.

That's when he almost passed out.

He grabbed for something to steady himself. As his head spun, he realized there was no air in the cellar. That's why the pilot didn't light. With some effort he climbed his way out of the cellar, holding tight to the stair railing, to get air.

"What's going on down there?" he asked Rosie, even though he could guess.

"Gary's making wine," she said.

The fermentation—those eighty-to-ninety-degree Fahrenheit bubbly burps—was eating up the air and replacing it with carbon dioxide. The cellar was filled with carbon dioxide. That's how much fermentation can eat up air in an enclosed space.

When the plumber revived, he went back down to the cellar and the first thing he did was open up a window. The cool autumn air rushed in and he could light the pilot.

When Gary got home, he was not happy.

"What's he doing? He could kill the fermentation."

He promptly closed the window.

It was the moment when Rosie faced her choices. She had two boys to raise. She had a career. Did she need this? Crushing grapes night and day? Fruit flies up the nose? No air to breathe? It's not that Gary was a bad guy or anything. No, he was a very decent guy. And he was a romantic. He wasn't afraid to show his emotions. And he cared for the boys. He took the time to do things with them. And they liked him, even though they thought he was a little strange with his wine thing. It was extreme. She had to laugh, it was so extreme.

But Rosie was smart. She knew she couldn't change a man. It's just not in the order of things. She would have to take him on his own terms. That's when she first got the idea that maybe they should build an addition to the garage for making wine. That would take care of the fruit flies. And extinguished pilot lights.

One day while rinsing dishes in the kitchen sink and staring out the window at her neighbor's side yard, she remembered her grandfather Nick. She always smiled at the memory of turning the tap on the oak barrel in the cellar and filling the pitcher for him with the wine. The hugs he gave. And she could feel the presence of some comforting ghost who wandered quietly in and out of her life. Gary was now a part of that.

That's when she realized that Gary had passed her test. Of course, to Gary, she had passed his. They married in 1989.

Outside spring was now on a tear, swaggering and rambunctious with youth under the late May sun.

Inside the winery, Gary said, "I want to show you something. I'll be right back."

He walked out of the winery into the tasting room and returned with a bottle of his 2007 Cabernet Franc and four wine glasses, which he placed on a table.

"Now come with me."

I followed as we walked down an aisle between the oak barrels stacked three high. Gary carried two of the empty glasses and a wine thief. Toward the back he turned into a smaller aisle, stuck his head between a bottom barrel and the one above, and withdrew the bung.

"This is the same vintage, but it's been in the barrel a year longer."

He withdrew some Cabernet Franc with the wine thief and filled both glasses. He placed the bung back in the barrel, and we returned to the folding table where we had left the other two glasses and the same bottled vintage. Now he filled the remaining glasses a quarter full with the Cab Franc from the bottle.

"Try the bottled Cab Franc first."

I swirled, drew in deeply the aroma, and drank.

"Good," I said.

"Now drink the wine from the barrel."

I swirled, drew in the aroma. It was fuller, richer. I drank.

The difference was startling. There was no doubt that the Cab Franc from the barrel was indeed fuller and had more body. The mouth responded to the greater fullness. And it stayed on the palate longer.

"It has more body, good mouthfeel, and length," Gary said, reading my thoughts.

While the bottled vintage was good, it was clear that longer aging in the barrel had made it better.

It's difficult for the uninitiated to appreciate how important aging is unless they can taste the same wine at different stages. Now *mouthfeel*, *length*, *depth*, *body*, and *fullness*—the wine vocabulary—came into perspective. *Fruit* and *bouquet* were still a bit of a challenge, but they, too, took on new meaning. The aging period is part of what the French call *elevage*. It's a difficult term to translate, but basically it has the same meaning one associates with raising children so that they become mature, refined adults.

"Can you taste the different fruit?" Gary asked.

Here is where I always had difficulty. My expression must have reflected that because Gary said, "It has good blueberry and cranberry."

His power of suggestion helped me to place it. He was right. There was the faintest hint of blueberry in the wine, although I did not get cranberry.

Again, Gary generally ages Cabernet Franc until just before the next harvest because he needs the barrels. In this instance it had been aging for eighteen months in the same barrel. For comparison, Merlot is aged, generally, at least twenty-four months in the barrel, and Cabernet Sauvignon thirty-three months.

Initially oak may have been selected simply for its utilitarian value as a container when it was first used in the Roman Empire, which learned the practice of making oak barrels from the German tribes. But over the centuries winemakers have learned how important it is as an ingredient and catalyst that makes subtle changes to the advantage of wine. Lactones, for example, provide the aroma associated with oak, which is sometimes also described as coconut. Phenolic aldehydes provide flavors such as vanilla. Volatile phenols result in spiciness associated with cloves or carnations. Then there is carbohydrate degradation that serves a function similar to how salt acts in bringing out flavor in meat. It can also provide bitter almond and caramel flavors. Tannins provide not only color but also astringency, the quality that makes your palate pucker with dryness and which I initially mistook for acidity. All of these features of oak contribute to and mix with the existing flavor compounds in the wine, creating new flavors.

But if oak can act as a condiment, the danger is that it can also mask flavors if it becomes too strong.

After we tasted the wine, Gary said: "This is not a fair comparison because every vintage is different. But come with me. Bring your glass."

I followed him to the other end of the winery to a barrel in the second row.

"This is the most recent Cabernet Franc."

I calculated that it had been aging for about six months. Certainly not optimum for a red. And it was true it was an entirely different vintage.

Gary pulled the bung, withdrew some wine with the wine thief, and poured it in my glass. He did the same for his.

We sniffed, and there was little aroma. We drank.

Highly acidic. No discernible fruit. Almost undrinkable. I didn't want to finish the glass, but Gary finished his so I finished mine. "Do you see what I mean?" he said, comparing it to the more maturely aged Cabernet Franc. "Aging brings out the fruit. It has more body. It's fuller and has more length. The tannins are less harsh. And oak is a big part of that. It imparts flavor."

Gary grows only vinifera grapes—again, Cabernet Franc, Chardonnay, Pinot Gris, and Riesling—which are European in origin. But you can make wine from American grape varieties. It's just not Gary's style. Not his philosophy. And one thing you learn is that winemakers have their own philosophies, often *strongly* held. Gary says he can drink American varietals and enjoy them when they are well made. But he adds a caveat: "You have to ask, why it is that for thousands of years winemakers have always made wine from *Vitis vinifera*" instead of American varieties such as *Vitis labrusca,* from which the common Concord grape is derived. "What is it about the taste? Winemaking reflects thousands of years of evolution to make the best wine."

This is reasonable. However, Europe simply didn't have *Vitis labrusca,* and by the time they were discovered (perhaps these were the grapes of Leif Erikson's Vinland in North America a thousand years ago) the *Vitis vinifera* and its taste were the established standard. The conventional wisdom—and not everyone agrees that it is indeed "wisdom"—is that American grapes simply make bad wine, or at least bad when placed next to the acquired taste associated with fine wines. The Concord taste is said to be "foxy." That's the equivalent of gaminess in meat. And if you enjoy wine that tastes like Welch's grape juice, which would be foxy, that may be okay.

Still, there are advocates, such as Chris Stamp, who believe American varietals have a place in the wine drinker's universe. In his newsletters, Stamp likes to pose with a machete in one hand and a bottle of his Lakewood Vineyards sparkling wine in the other, decapitating the bottle to enjoy the vintage. It's part of the playfulness Stamp exhibits on the job as the winemaker at his family-owned Lakewood, one of the older artisanal wineries in the Finger Lakes, founded in 1980.

If nothing else, the playfulness helps counter Chris's high energy—he is always on the run at the winery, which sits above the southwest side of Seneca Lake, not far from Watkins Glen where the famous race-car track is. His is one of the Finger Lakes wineries that still makes wine from American varietals. In his case, he makes it from Concord, Delaware, and Niagara grapes. That makes him a challenger of the conventional *vinifera* wisdom. Contrary to it, he believes there is a market for the taste of such wines—although he admits that he too prefers *vinifera* wines, which he also makes. But he defends those who like going native.

"A lot of people come through the door who like *labrusca*," he told me one rainy afternoon while we sat around the table in his conference room tasting his Delaware and Concord. He reminded me of a studious prep school boy behind his wire-rimmed glasses, perhaps because his high energy overflows with studious intensity. Except that he tends to wear hiking shoes, shorts, a light, neon-blue tee shirt with the Lakewood logo over his heart, and to wield a machete when he poses for the newsletter. What is clear is that he's not into convention.

"I don't know why *labrusca* is looked down on so much," he lamented.

Part of it he sees as cultural: Tastes change. For example, he notes that Nicholas Longworth, who hailed from Cincinnati and has been called the father of American wine, made sparkling pink Catawba (from the American Catawba grape) back in the nineteenth century from grapes grown in his vineyards along the Ohio River Valley. ("Ohio was once the wine capital of the country," Chris said.) It was certainly one of the most popular wines in the United States in its day. It was the favorite wine of the English poet Robert Browning. And the American poet Henry Wadsworth Longfellow sang its praises in a poem he published in 1858 called "This Song of Mine is a Song of the Vine," Stamp said. And now the winemaker cum laude recited passages from the poem to me from memory:

> …Catawba wine
> Has a taste more divine,
> More dulcet, delicious, and dreamy.

What is striking about the poem is its nineteenth-century catalog of native American grape varieties, with a special place reserved for the Catawba grown along the banks of the "Beautiful River," the Ohio. The poem must surely be the only one dedicated to singing the praises of an American varietal wine. And certainly it supports Stamp's point of view that tastes change over time. After all, European wines—*Vitis vinifera*—are accused in the poem of racking "ones brains With the fever Pains," so much so that Longfellow urges, "To the sewers and sinks With all such drinks," and characterizes "Borgia"—Italian wines—the "Devil's Elixir."

"When pink Catawba was in its zenith," Stamp said, "Longworth accused questionable New York restaurants with filling his empty bottles with cheap French Champagne." Champagne, clearly, was déclassé. *Touché*, Dom Perignon.

There is also, Stamp admitted, a pragmatic business side to making *labrusca*-based wines. "It gives me the opportunity to spread my eggs out in different baskets." In one deadly freeze in 2004, many vineyards saw significant losses of *vinifera* vines. Even Riesling, which is more cold hearty than, say, Merlot or Cabernet Sauvignon, saw a high mortality rate.

"Since then, a lot more people have been making wine out of Niagara," he said. A consequence is that while there was very little competition for Niagara before then, "I have to do more promotion now to make my Niagara sell."

So, who buys American varietals? Some suggest, based on informed speculation, that it depends on the age of the buyer. Alice Peters, an assistant manager at one of the largest wine retailers in Upstate New York, said that there's an older generation that always imbibed the native wine.

"When younger people come in they say they're getting it for their mother or their grandfather. They act as if they're ashamed. You're talking about buyers in their forties or fifties," she said.

I recall my father, in the late 1950s or early 1960s, buying a Taylor Lake Country red in a nice wine bottle with a screw top (now you usually buy it in a box) as a gift for his hosts when invited over for supper. That, to him, was a good, uncontroversial wine. But life was simpler back then, and with less pretense. French wines were only for a certain elite class to which my parents didn't aspire, and wouldn't have known how to aspire even if they wanted.

Alice, however, thinks there is a more compelling reason than just the demographics of age: "Price point. That's important to people, the price."

And as another wine buyer told me, there is a generation of younger wine drinkers who buy the wine because "America is still a soda pop culture."

Alice agrees. "It's sweet and it tastes like grape juice."

Dana Malley, the store's general manager and principal wine buyer adds still one more reason. "It seems to be more of a local phenomenon," he said. There's a tradition in Upstate New York and throughout the Northeast. But while there is an older generation which has always imbibed *labrusca* wines, he said he hears from wineries around the region that young people buy it, too.

"It's not uncommon for a young person to buy not only a Cab Franc, but to walk out with a more sweet *labrusca*," Malley said. "I see it with students from Cornell. They don't have as many preconceptions. They don't have the attitude that this, this, and this is good, and that this, this, and this is bad the way fine wine drinkers do. They are less prone to attach certain images to wines."

Chris Stamp agreed. A testament to the popularity of American varietals is Red Cat, he said, made by Hazlitt 1852 Vineyards and Winery between Seneca and Cayuga lakes. By far the most sold New York State wine—in 2008 they sold nearly a hundred thousand cases of the wine—it is indeed a sweet wine without pretense, made from Catawba grapes, from whence it derives its name. Of course, part of its popularity is due no doubt to its marketing slogan, which employees and wine tasters alike chant at the winery: "Red Cat, Red Cat, it's an aphrodisiac. Red Cat, Red Cat, it'll get you in the sack!" Perhaps not surprisingly, Hazlitt, which is widely known as a party winery, also sells Red Cat thongs.

In cool spring air during the third week in May, Joe held an eight-foot wooden post upright in his hands. He could feel the earth-shaking vibration as the hydraulic post driver crashed down atop the post with a reverberating bang. This was his second year at Long Point. Under a gray sky that occasionally flashed the memory of sun in a silver seam, there was only the dull, repetitive hammering of the red hydraulic post driver bolted to the John Deere tractor pounding the post into the damp earth still wet from a light rain the night before.

While Thom Bechtold, a vineyard hand on loan from King Ferry Winery, operated the post driver from beneath a floppy hat, Joe maintained his grip on the post between both gloved hands. His hands ached from the vibration that shivered through the trembling timber every time the hydraulic hammer dropped. The vineyard was scattered with pointed posts still to be set—giant, eight-foot pencils scattered by some playful Bacchus across the landscape. The vines were staked the first year the way you might stake a tomato plant. Indeed, until the posts were erected, the staked vines looked from a distance like a field of tomato plants.

From the posts, galvanized steel fruiting wires would be attached, and from the wires the Cabernet Franc plantings will someday cling as they reach up for sunlight during the summer.

The vines had now leafed and were eight to eighteen inches high and just as broad, depending on how well they survived the winter. This was nothing compared to the fulsomeness they would have in maturity when, in a couple years and with luck, the vines would be thick with the grape, which is nearly black in color.

"The soil is pretty shallow. Gary put in a row of experimental vines first. They're doing pretty good," Joe said as he and Thom prepared to drive another post. Thom drove the tractor over twenty feet and positioned the hydraulic hammer above the spot marked for the next post. As Joe walked over he rubbed his aching hands. At the highest point of the vineyard next to Lake Road the experimental row rose two-thirds up the trellis. They were well on their way to providing a first small— but highly symbolic—crop of red grapes this season.

Joe motioned to Bechtold with his hand to shift the post driver over about six inches.

"Stop," he yelled, his voice just barely audible above the grinding of the tractor motor, and he held up his hand to illustrate the command. He picked up the post, wrapping both hands around it, and wrestled it into position until it was upright to the eye. "Okay!" he

yelled. The weight of the post driver rose. Joe nodded, and, like an afterthought, the weight dropped in another earth-trembling bang. The sound echoed metallically against the nearby sheet metal barn on the neighboring farm.

A few days later at Long Point, the posts stood upright in two and a half feet of soil and projected five and a half above ground. The spring was turning out to be a rainy one, but today the sun was out and Joe's eyes squinted in the bright light as he focused and pounded a large steel staple into the side of a post with a carpenter's hammer. Between the prongs of the staple ran a fruiting wire. The stake shuddered with each blow.

The temperature was in the high sixties. The surface of Cayuga Lake, beyond the horizon of the recently mowed field and the distant line of forest, shimmered when the sun broke through a passing cloud.

Most modern vineyards use rows of wire trellises for trellising grapes—this is usually what we see from the roadside or in those postcards of Bordeaux or the Rhine. But it is not the only means used in the long history of wine-grape growing. In ancient Syria, Egypt, and Greece an early favored method was to train the vines up trees. The vines could also be cultivated in festoons draping from tree limb to tree limb. A medieval wood block print shows a vine climbing up a tree trunk and passing through a hole in the center of the tree to the other side. Another ancient method still used in remote vineyards in southern Italy is to let the vines grow on the ground into thick bushes. Vines can also be staked from low trellises close to the ground. That is how it is done on the Côte d'Or and in the Loire in France, with vines rising only about three feet. Then there are the courtyard pergolas from Roman times that served as shade arbors, which today have made a comeback in the backyards of the *House Beautiful* set. The classical Greeks probably introduced modern trellising as we know it, although growing vines up trees long continued as a practice.

June is a time when the vineyardist thins and trains shoots, which seem to grow inches a day. During thinning and training one learns intimately about the personality of the grapevine. It is a strange creature and one can see why in ancient Greece and Rome it represented the cycles of life. The bark on the main trunk tends to be cracked and crumpled, hanging in threads in some places, and reminiscent of a withered old man. It's not pretty to look at. But the vine comes to life in the smooth brown canes that were young growth the year before, and then in the tender, rubbery green shoots of the current season.

Joe reached out with his gloved hand to rake across the bottom of the vines, stripping the leaves away to provide more sunlight for the nascent berries.

The vineyard at Long Point slopes gently. The reason you so often see vineyards on hillsides is because slopes help to circulate air under the canopy of vine leaves. If the land is flat, you get little natural air movement. Because of the slope, warm air rises, and cool air sinks. Air movement helps to flush the vineyard of mold spores and provide air drainage in winter months so that cold air will keep moving and not freeze the buds.

Long Point's Cabernet Franc vineyard at the top of the hill overlooking the winery is a symbol of Gary's love for red wine. More than anything, Gary was committed to making red wine when he started the winery. Dry red wine, no less. That's where the challenge begins. Because, at the verge of the Canadian Shield, the Finger Lakes tend to be white wine country.

Gary chose Cabernet Franc grapes because of their hardiness and because they can be harvested earlier than Cabernet Sauvignon. They are probably the best red *Vitis vinifera* for growing in the Finger Lakes.

There's a climatic distinction between reds and whites. Reds do better in the dry, warmer regions of the Mediterranean. Whites tend to do better more to the north. That's why the best wines from the Rhine region in Germany are usually white, say Riesling or Gewürztraminer. This is also why the Finger Lakes have the reputation for making Rieslings that are competitive with German and Alsatian Rieslings. As Rod Smith, a wine critic for *Wine & Spirits Magazine,* once noted, "The Finger Lakes region is quite similar to the best viticultural areas of Germany's Mosel, Saar-Ruwer, Nahe and Rhine river valleys. The combination of deep, narrow lakes and steep bordering ridges particularly resembles the mid-Mosel district, site of some of the world's greatest Riesling vineyards.... The ridges provide meager, well-drained soils, angled exposure to the sun and frost-preventing air drainage. The lakes regulate the local climate by tempering the seasonal extremes." The result is that "Finger Lakes Rieslings can stand with the world's best."

While European red wine grapes are difficult to grow in the Finger Lakes, Cabernet Franc is an exception. (Pinot Noir of Burgundy fame is another, but Gary doesn't grow them because he says he's not impressed with the clones available for the Finger Lakes.) The Cabernet Franc also has a curious heritage. It is the parent of the better-known Cabernet Sauvignon, which is a cross, one likely engineered by nature and not man, between Cabernet Franc and Sauvignon Blanc in the eighteenth century, perhaps when a stray stamen escaped the orbit of its ovary and drifted off to the ovary of the different varietal. In France Cabernet Franc tends to be lighter in body. Gary vints a full-bodied version in the California style. Admittedly, it is not as popular as its child, Cabernet Sauvignon. But if you want to have a taste of the past, say of the time of the Three Musketeers, close your eyes and sip a Cabernet Franc.

The year Gary planted the Chardonnay, 1999, he also had the experimental section for the Cabernet Franc plowed and underground drainage installed to carry off excess rain. He knew the location was important: It was what motorists would see first on New York State Route 90 when they approached from either direction: a vineyard where ripe grapes would hang in pendulous black clusters, provocative to the eye and the imagination. That picture of a vineyard and grape clusters, an image lodged in human consciousness for thousands of years as a symbol of the earth's fecundity, would serve as both the introduction to and frame for the winery situated a little way down the hill. Beyond it would be more vineyards, then the verge of forest and Cayuga Lake glittering in its glacial valley. The location would say: Come in, we're the winery of your dreams.

The experimental section of Cabernet Franc weathered the first two winters well. "I needed a safe bet that wasn't going to die off," Gary said. Cabernet Franc is not without its risks, however. "It has to have total ripeness. Cabernet Sauvignon, if not ripe, is still workable." Still, Gary opted for the reasonably safe bet.

After those first two summers Gary decided he couldn't be both winemaker and vineyardist, so he hired Joe. One of Joe's first jobs was to prepare the rest of the Cabernet Franc field for planting. While he waited for his Cabernet to mature, Gary made wine with other grower's grapes, which he bought in the region, across the state, as well as from California when necessary.

But once the vines matured, Gary confronted a marketing dilemma he had not anticipated. The lesser-known Cabernet Franc was not selling well. "I've got too many varieties. I think the Cab Franc gets lost in the shuffle," he said. Simply, Cabernet Franc doesn't have the kind of cachet that Chardonnay has, or Cabernet Sauvignon, Merlot, and Syrah. At the time, he seriously considered using Cab Franc for what they generally are used for, at least in the United States—blending and *vin ordinaire*. "Moon Puppy is a good alternative use," he said, referring to his sweet red wine made for the majority of wine drinkers who prefer wine that way. Eventually, he would change his mind. It would prove to be one more step in the learning curve.

 SUMMER

FINALLY SUMMER — LATE JUNE, on time, the sequel to a short spring, the increasing heat of the sun leaving the earth warm to the touch in the evenings.

The vines flower. Except that grapevines flower all but unnoticed to the untrained eye. Unlike colorful fruit varieties—apple, cherry, for example—grape flowers are small, green, and underwhelming.

The flowers lose their caps, and the stamens are freed, most of them drifting on the breeze to pollinate the neighboring ovary. Only about 30 percent of the flowers are successfully pollinated. But flowering is one more tentative measure of the future crop. If there are few flowers, perhaps because of winter damage, the crop will be small.

Dan removed a secondary cane missed in earlier pruning and tucked in a stray shoot. Occasionally, he stripped morning glory vines at the base of the trunks, although he knew he was going to have to spray for the pest. The thick green sward in the alleyways between the trellises was speckled with the white flower, providing a colorful accent to the canopy of green grapevines. But the morning glory is no friend of grapes. Permitted to grow around the roots, it can choke off and strangle the vine. Spraying is the only thing that will kill it.

For now, however, Dan focused on removing excess shoots because they, too, rob the plant of nutrients, as well as provide too much shade and so delay maturing.

Working in the vineyard is a curious, soothing kind of work surrounded every day by head-high walls of green. Below the rise of the hillock that looks out on the lake you feel boxed in by the green walls framing the arching blue universe above. One of the challenges working in the vineyard is to keep the mind occupied.

"I thought I was going to go crazy when I started working by myself," Dan said. Now he takes his iPod with him and listens to recorded talk shows to keep his mind occupied. Sometimes he gets so involved in the discussions that they become more of a reality than the surrounding vineyard. Like the time he listened to someone on a radio talk show discuss how important it is to tell those you love that you love them before they are gone. Suddenly, tears welled in Dan's eyes as he pruned spurs. He took out his cell phone, called his mother, and told her he loved her.

More recently, Levi Valez-Reed, a graduate of Wells College in nearby Aurora, has worked with Dan on a part-time basis, as well as over at King Ferry Winery, where he works with Dan's wife, Lindsay. When Dan and Levi work together, they often get into lengthy discussion. And it can get heated—such as the time they took up opposing views on abortion, two young men stubbornly adhering to the standard script as the national debate played out amid the grape vines.

While Gary knew how to make wine when he opened the winery in 1999, he had never grown wine grapes before. It proved to be one more lesson.

First, he hired a contractor to place underground drainage pipe. The contractor plowed the field with a chisel plow that busted up the rocky earth. He removed the rocks and brought in a backhoe to dig the three-foot-deep drainage trenches. He laid the black flexible pipe and covered it over.

Gary personally staked out the vine rows and attached a string between the first row. He took spray cans of white paint and painstakingly painted the ground traversed by the string. Then he moved the string up one row and did the same. When he finished he laid out lateral rows and painted them yellow. Where white and yellow lines intersected, he would plant vines. Pete Saltonstall, again the owner of

nearby King Ferry Winery, brought his tractor over and a tree planter. While Pete drove the tractor at a walking pace, Gary sat atop the tree planter, which is like a harness-racing sulky. The planter plowed a small trench, and when Gary rode over where white and yellow lines intersected, he placed the grape plant in the trench. Wheels under the planter oriented in a V shape pushed the dirt back into the trench, and the grapevine was planted.

Planting the vineyard was no easy task that summer because the season was one of the hottest on record. "It was so hot it fried the finish off the hood of my pickup," Gary said. Corn crops in neighboring fields shriveled and turned brown, then a bleached-out yellow.

"Do I need to water the plants?" Gary asked Pete before they planted.

"Nah. We get more than enough rain around here in summer," Gary recalls Pete telling him.

Gary asked because of where his winery is located: water in any quantity is too deep and expensive to drill for. He did drill a shallow well, but that could easily run dry and he had to conserve water for the public restrooms. So eventually he planned to have water shipped in by truck. But it was their first year, money was tight, and they would try to do without.

During a normal summer they do have enough rain. Plus, grapevines like dry weather. But that year was too hot and dry. It was like a Saharan sirocco, with a hot, dry wind, had settled over Upstate. A few days after they planted the vines, Pete called Gary.

"I think you better water."

"Water? How am I going to do that?"

"I don't know, but you better water."

Here was Gary, with a newly planted vineyard, and he had to water it with water he didn't have.

The first thing he did was take ten- and fifteen-gallon plastic containers down to the state park nearby on the lake. He went to the shower rooms. Occasionally, on really hot days, he would go to the state park to take showers to cool down. He filled up the buckets, went back to the vineyard, and watered the plants. He watered every one of the 1,100 grapevines by hand, making countless trips down to the state park to get water.

As his brain bubbled under the parching sun there were times when he couldn't distinguish between what was real and what was illusion. One day while he was in the vineyard watering the plants he received a call on his cell phone from Rosie.

"Did you hear that John Kennedy Jr. was killed?" she said.

"You've got to be kidding me! Holy crow!"

As the brain cells simmered and steamed in the glare of the sun Gary had an eerie sense of being back in the sixth grade and 1963 when President Kennedy was assassinated. There was a sense that the past was more real and that the present had become a mirage in the desert. He looked at the wilting grapevines, the cracked, baked earth, and could only shake his head. For a moment he couldn't help but conclude that his dream of a winery was just a mirage. What the hell was he doing, trying to start a winery at middle age?

Sometimes he took one of the plastic buckets of water and poured it over his head. And the water seemed to be a mirage, too. When he was more clear-minded, he realized he couldn't wait another year to get water. He talked with a water supplier who sold water by the tank load.

"Get a 1,500-gallon tank. You can get one from Farm Tractor Supply. Don't get a 1,000-gallon tank. I deliver 1,100 gallons, so you'll lose 100 gallons. Get a 1,500 gallon," the supplier told him.

Gary took off from work one day and went to the local Farm Tractor Supply in Cortland. All they had were 1,000-gallon tanks.

"I need a 1,500-gallon tank."

"We don't have any."

"How long will it take to get one."

"Maybe there's one at our store in Auburn."

They called, and there was. It was about a forty-five-minute drive.

At the Auburn Farm Tractor Supply he bought a 1,500-gallon plastic tank.

"I've got to go rent a Ryder truck. I'll be back in a little while to pick it up," he told the checkout clerk.

He rented the truck, but when he returned to Farm Tractor Supply, he discovered the truck was too small. He went back to Ryder and got a bigger truck.

"And that one was too small, too," he said.

It was one of those moments when he asked himself, "What have I gotten myself into?"

He called his water supplier, who was due to make a delivery and told him what happened.

"I know a guy who has a truck it will fit on and he'll pick it up and deliver it for a hundred bucks," the supplier said.

"I've already flushed a hundred bucks down the toilet and have nothing to show for it. Go ahead and do it."

That's how Gary got water at the winery. And his grapes were watered.

Then, during that endlessly long, hot summer, he had to spray the plants with fungicide. In one-hundred-degree plus temperatures he dressed up in a Tyvek chemical suit, respirator and goggles, and donned a back sprayer. As he went from plant to plant spraying, and as the temperature in the suit rose so he was suffocating in a mist of perspiration, it was all he could do to keep from passing out.

But the vines survived.

At a booth under a long tent, hands holding souvenir wine glasses thrust out in eager supplication for a blessing. My wine lapped over the edge of the glass from the jostling crowd. No one apologized. When I tried to pull back from the counter to get out of the way, the packed, sweating bodies of other wine drinkers seeking to have their glasses filled pressed from behind. Amid the heat and the crush, the Finger Lakes Wine Festival took on a frenzied quality as people chugged wine with the kind of gusto one expected of beer drinkers at an Oktoberfest celebration. I found it difficult to concentrate on the taste with all the jostling. I missed the quiet of a civilized tasting room, where you can look out and reflect on a calm lake lying in its valley.

The annual festival is the premier event of the wine season in Upstate New York and is held in Watkins Glen in July at the race-car track. Finger Lakes wineries set up booths and present their wines to an admission-paying public. It's like an annual coming-out party when many new vintages are released.

Yet, it seemed contrary to the intimate nature of wine, I thought, my senses overwhelmed by the pounding percussion of the bluegrass and reggae bands on a stage under a stand of trees, the smells of frying sausage and peppers, and those of the fried dough stand. At little café tables enophiles sipped wine or Pepsi. The July sun was wilting and the neighboring hills of Upstate steamed in the humidity. I found I wanted a cold beer.

Later, some fifty wine aficionados sat stiffly at banks of tables under a tent. In front of each sat four glasses of Chardonnay to taste, as well as wafers and pitchers of water for cleansing palates and some dump jars.

"There's a saying that Riesling is 99 percent made in the vineyard. But Chardonnay is different," said Chris Stamp, the winemaker from Lakewood Vineyards on Seneca Lake. Now, instead of the earnest student, he was the energetic showman, the kind that lops off Champagne bottles with a machete. "Chardonnay comes into the winery screwed up."

That's why it benefits from the winemaker's art.

"What I want you to do is taste each wine and rate how much oak you think it has," Stamp declared. "Each one has been aged differently. And one of the Chardonnays was aged only in stainless steel so it has no oak."

People took five minutes, others ten, to sniff their Chardonnay and take long sips. Some looked at the ceiling of the tent as they reflected. Others stared at their glasses. Some spat and used their dump jars. Slowly, tentatively, they wrote down their responses.

Finally, Chris announced: "The first has oak. The second none. The third has oak. And the fourth has oak."

How the different Chardonnay were aged was revealing, like the way there are different recipes for making the same dish. On the one hand, Vinny Aliperti, the winemaker at Atwater Estate Vineyards, explained that he aged only in oak and stirred the lees about once every four weeks. Stamp, on the other hand, did not stir the lees and aged his Chardonnay in oak for about ten months. John McGregor, the owner and winemaker at McGregor Vineyard and Winery above Keuka Lake, aged only about 30 percent of his Chardonnay in barrels and 70 percent in stainless steel. After seven months he blended the two.

"I don't like to oversaturate with oak," he said.

Other nuances of the winemaker's art emerged. McGregor used new French barrels for his. That alone was reason for not aging all of his Chardonnay in new oak because of the heady savor of the new wooden barrels.

After the tasting, outside the tent, I confronted the same jostling, heat, and difficulty focusing on the taste of a vintage.

I told Gary my impression of the wine festival. He recalled one young man, probably barely of drinking age, who thrust his souvenir glass through the arms of other tasters.

"What do you want?" Gary asked.

"Anything you got."

"I couldn't believe it," Gary said. "All he wanted to do was get drunk."

Later, down the tent at another winery's booth, there was chanting—"One, two, three, four," followed by a loud whoop from what sounded like a crowd of young people engaged in a fraternity ritual.

A tasting counter employee by the name of Steven, who does promotions for another winery, showed up. Gary and Steven know each other from the wine-tasting circuit. Steven was taking a break from his winery's tasting table in the exhibition hall next door. He had deep-set eyes covered with smoky glasses and a luxuriantly thick black beard.

"We just released another red. You ought to try it," Gary said above the din of pressing wine tasters, the whoops, the rituals. "You really ought to try it."

Steven tried it.

"You know, I like this more than ours. I like oak in my red," he said. "And this has oak."

Different philosophies.

Another loud whoop sounded. It split the air from about fifty feet away, a whoop that had been punctuating the air for the last half hour. It dawned on everyone all at once.

"There's something going on down there," Gary said.

"Maybe they have to have a party because their wine is so bad," Steven said. "I know. I used to work for them."

"This had twenty-two Brix," Gary said, referring to the measure of sugar content in the grapes that went into the strongly oaked red. Steven nodded knowingly. Twenty-two was good sugar content.

The whoop sounded again. Margaret, Gary's tasting assistant and recent graduate of Wells College, went over to find out why. She returned with a report of youthful revelers quaffing wine with the gusto one associates with drinking beer at an Oktoberfest celebration.

The bacchanal continued with another whoop.

"Bacchanal, *noun:* drunken revelry or carousal."

Always, Bacchus, the riotous Greek and Roman god of wine, seemed to lurk in the shadows of wine and its culture—paradoxical, enigmatic, intriguing. Like wine. Perhaps because the ancient conception was one in which he was more than just the god of wine. Or rather, wine was more than just the fruit of the vine, containing, like the god's personality, many contradictory facets. Also known as Dionysus to the Greeks, he was the god of ecstasy. But he was equally the god of mayhem. He represented fertility, and he could be the instrument of death. He cared for his devotees, the satyrs and bacchae, when they engaged in their frenzied bacchanals, when they indulged what we now call Dionysian appetites. But if humans refused to acknowledge the divinity of the god of wine—and by implication their own paradoxical nature, the ecstatic and the chaotic—Bacchus arranged so their own actions resulted in their destruction. One thing Bacchus was not: a rational god, even if the Greeks did invent rational philosophy. So it was in wine and not only in the calculations of the rational mind, the ancient Greeks believed, that you could achieve profound illumination about the human condition.

That's why the notion of *in vino veritas*—in wine there is truth—derives from the Greeks. The earliest reference to it is from Alcaeus, a Greek poet who lived about 600 BC and who, among other accomplishments, wrote drinking songs. In one of his surviving fragments, he notes: "Wine, dear boy, and truth." From what little we know about Alcaeus, he was a lush.

The classical symposium was the venue for the search for truth in wine, and not infrequently it turned into a riotous bacchanal. While today it may be associated with dreary lectures by stuffy college professors in overheated classrooms under the glare of fluorescent lights, the true classical symposium was in some ways more like the Finger Lakes Wine Festival. In classical Greek, "symposium" translated as "drinking party." It was, admittedly, a more sedate affair when its members initially gathered: Around a *kratur* or large bowl or basin of wine, men would lie languorously on couches, or *clinai*, with an arm over a pillow to prop the head as they drank from their wine bowls. The event was presided over by the *symposiarch*, elected in democratic fashion by the assembled. The Greeks diluted their wine with water, a practice still found today in modern Greece, and the *symposiarch* would determine how much water to add to the wine. Frequently, the symposium was attended by youthful dancers and musicians playing flute and lyre. With the mild intoxicant the participants of the symposium would find their minds mildly elevated, and they would engage in metaphysical discussion in the search for truth. "Rise up above the troubles, and with me / Drink in a cloud of blossoms," is how Euripedes describes the wine-induced pleasure of the symposium. Under its influence, according to Aeschylus, "Wine is the mirror of the soul."

But Dionysus's gift to man involved more than just metaphysics. As Philochorus notes: "People who are drinking wine reveal not only their inner being but also everything else, observing no restrictions in speech." One result was frat house camaraderie. Because of such wine-induced compulsion the staid preliminaries of the symposium could metamorphose into still something else. As Bacchylides said in the fifth century BC: "Dionysus mingles in the wine new powers, / Sending high adventure to the thoughts of men." Often such thoughts of high adventure resulted in a debauch as the men became enamored with the dancing and flute girls, and sometimes with the serving boys, and sometimes with themselves. The frat house drinking orgy was born. This is why the symposium has always had the lingering smell of a disreputable enterprise, despite the veneer of academic propriety. If wine still has a role in today's academic symposium, it is perhaps in the professorial pose of the wine glass in elevated hand passing for the ecstasy of erudition—or the indecipherable mutterings of intellectual mayhem.

When Gary and Margaret closed up for the day, Gary took a bucket of ice outside to dump. Margaret wiped off the display table. An older man with a bloated face and stomach and a balding, gray pate shuffled up to the table. His cheeks and nose were flushed with red capillary veins. He asked Margaret in a soft, gentle voice as he extended his wine glass, "May I?" and his voice trailed off, sensing, I think, that the hour was late and he was afraid he might cause some unintended offense; it was as if he wanted to withdraw his request the moment it escaped from his lips so that he wouldn't have to endure Margaret's gentle rebuff, with a kind smile, "I'm sorry. We don't have any more open bottles."

Quietly, he shuffled off with a disappointed smile. Eventually, Bacchus, too, must sober up.

Now the neighboring farm fields were rich with alfalfa green and the paler green of young corn. It was high summer as I surveyed the countryside out the window from Rosie's office over the tasting room.

"We should have called it the seat-of-our-pants winery," she said.

In a sense, starting the winery depended on a bet between Rosie and Gary.

As his amateur winemaking improved, Gary began floating the idea to Rosie. "Maybe I should start a winery. What do you think?"

This was in the mid-1990s.

At first it was just a dream, Gary admits, no more than a flight of fancy. But as he won more awards, he kept saying, "Yeah, maybe I should start a winery."

Slowly, the idea germinated, and finally, out of exasperation, Rosie said, "I tell you what, Gar. If you win a gold medal for a white wine you can start your winery."

She had a reason.

"Well, what about the red ones?" he said.

"No. If you start a winery you have to make both reds and whites. And your whites suck."

It was an instance of her being his toughest critic.

"I always liked them," he responded.

As an amateur winemaker he had made white Muscat, Chardonnay, Chenin Blanc, and Sauvignon Blanc.

"My friends liked them," he told me. "But she would say, 'Your whites suck.' Literally." Rosie wasn't being entirely fair because she doesn't care for white wine anyway. While she will taste, she won't drink them. "I have never seen her order a white wine in a restaurant, yet," Gary said. Except for Champagne. But Champagne is Champagne.

Anyway, she thought she had trumped her husband. His flights of fancy were beginning to sprout wings. It was time to clip them.

He thought otherwise.

In 1997 he made a Chardonnay with grapes from King Ferry Winery. Admittedly, it was a superlative year for grapes. "It was just a beautiful crop. I've never seen a more beautiful crop," Gary said.

He entered the Chardonnay in an American Wine Society competition.

"She didn't think I was going to win," Gary said.

They drove to the Society's annual convention, in Pittsburgh that year, where they attended seminars on grape growing and wine tasting. And they attended the awards ceremony. When the Society announced the winners in the amateur winemaking competition, they started with the bronze for Chardonnay.

Gary didn't win.

They announced the silver.

He didn't win.

Then came the gold, and everyone knew that there would be no also-rans.

"And for the gold," the announcer said, looking at his card, "the winner is Gary Barletta."

Gary and Rosie looked at each other, stunned. Then, like the rising sun, Gary's triumphant grin spread across his face. His whites suck?

"I can't believe it," Rosie said, but not because she had lost the bet.

"She was jumping up and down," Gary said. "She was thrilled."

As he walked up to accept the award, he passed the table where Ellie Harkness Butz was sitting. Ellie was then an enologist at Purdue University and the founder of the Indiana International Wine Competition, another important competition among amateur winemaking circles and one in which Gary has also won awards. Earlier at the conference Gary had told Ellie about the bet with Rosie.

Now, as Gary walked by Ellie—as he recalls—she said, "I guess you're going to open your winery now."

The award was the divine sign from the Wine Society that they needed.

There was something else, too, Gary said: "Rosie likes challenges."

If they were going to open a winery, it soon became clear that they needed a business plan. In 1998 Rosie wrote one. At the time she was studying for her MBA at LeMoyne College in Syracuse. She decided to write the plan as her master's thesis.

"The hardest part was the 'what ifs,'" she said. "My professor would play devil's advocate and keep asking, 'What if this happens? What if that happens?'"

Gary first saw the property he wanted in 1997. He had been working as a part-time volunteer at King Ferry to learn the winery business, and Pete Saltonstall told him about some property for sale with a view of the lake, property that might be a good site for a winery. "Wow," was Gary's reaction when he saw it, sloping away toward a line of trees, with the lake in the distance. "Beautiful piece of property. I like the southwesterly exposure. It's all cleared. No trees to remove. It's ready for planting."

The view would be important for customers—the lake sweeping before you. If you were a Finger Lakes winery, you had to have a lake view.

Getting a loan for the property was easy compared to the loan they would need for building the winery. In 1998 the Barlettas bought seven acres for $25,000. Or, rather, Gary bought it because Rosie had already used her house as collateral for loans on her sons' college educations.

"It was hysterical they gave him the loan for the land because he didn't own anything. He never had any debts. He didn't even have a credit rating," Rosie said. Gary's talent for avoiding long-term financial commitments, something he prides himself on, paid off: He qualified for a loan.

Now came the most challenging part, building the winery. They needed the business plan because they had gone to a couple of banks seeking loans and were asked, Do you have any savings? Do you have an inheritance? Stocks? What collateral do you have? "Collateral? What collateral?" Rosie said. "All we have is a house in Cortland I bought in 1983 for $39,900. That's it."

Loan officers would ask what they had in the way of capital equipment.

"We had a hand crusher. We had two ancient presses. We had four barrels—two of them were new and I thought that was pretty exciting."

That's when Gary and Rosie realized they would have to sell themselves with the business plan—and, most important, sell the idea that the winery was viable as a business.

At the heart of the plan was the winery's location. To the north, by two miles, lay the village of Aurora, home to Wells College, then an exclusive women's college founded by the Wells half of Wells Fargo back in the nineteenth century. Just as important, on the north end of the village sat MacKenzie-Childs, a manufacturer of high-end household furnishings for the upscale Birkenstock set. They had a store, a restaurant serving American nouvelle cuisine, and a wealthy clientele. Then in the village there was the Aurora Inn. Built in 1833, it was a handsome piece of nineteenth-century Americana out of a Currier & Ives print that once served as a stagecoach stop. It had a restaurant catering to both the MacKenzie-Childs crowd and the parents of the college students.

Down the side road that served as the entrance to Long Point Winery lay Long Point State Park with a boat landing. The boating crowd had to pass the winery to get to water. By necessity they had expensive tastes. Maybe, just maybe, they would forgo beer for the voyage and buy wine instead.

Finally, about four miles south of the land sat King Ferry Winery. It was a well-established winery and it was an accepted fact of marketing that wineries close to each other created marketing synergy: They became more attractive as destinations for enophiles because of their proximity.

It looked like a good plan.

"But what if?" Rosie's professor asked, looking at her dubiously. He was not dubious out of malice. But he knew the kind of challenges Gary and Rosie could face. He listened to many students' dreams, and he had to prepare them for the realities of starting a business. He wanted to forearm them against the kind of business misfortunes they could confront.

What if, for example, MacKenzie-Childs, as was rumored, opened a new and bigger store in New York City? What would be the impact locally?

What if the Aurora Inn went bankrupt?

And so it went, the professor chipping away at the basis for the winery's possible success. At one point Rosie had to do a presentation to her class, and she did it on how to make homemade pasta, one of her specialties. The professor said, "I think you're going to have more success making pasta than building a winery."

At first the bank loan officers were incredulous. "That's your business plan?" one asked. Rosie could tell from the wrinkle on his brow what he was thinking: You're crazy. She got a curt, professional smile, the noncommittal kind, and never heard from him again.

Over time, after more visits to bank loan officers, Rosie refined the plan, responding to the what-ifs. And the plan grew. Initially, the plan was two pages long. The final plan was thirty-six pages long.

"My first business plan was a dream. It was about our dream. My last business plan was a financial accomplishment. It said, this is what we're going to achieve, and how we're going to get there."

They kept applying to banks. They kept getting rejected. It became an exercise in humiliation. They eventually applied to thirteen banks, and it was at lucky thirteen that they found a loan officer who was willing to believe in their dream, too.

The sympathetic loan officer, John Halleron, worked at Alternatives Federal Credit Union in Ithaca. The locale says a lot. Ithaca, New York, is an unusual place. The home of Cornell University and Ithaca College, the town is a throwback to a more liberal era. It's the kind of place that's been known to elect a socialist mayor. It's the home of the famous vegetarian Moosewood Restaurant. It even has its own currency measured in Ithaca Hours that many businesses accept because, well, it's Ithaca. And in conservative Upstate New York, Ithaca is referred to with a mixture of fondness and loathing as The People's Republic of Ithaca. After all, Alternatives Federal Credit Union is an *alternative* credit union.

As Rosie and Gary recall, Halleron was intrigued by the idea of the winery. Gary could tell when he walked into his office.

"You make wine? You really make wine?" Halleron asked.

"Yeah. I make wine," Gary said, suggesting, well, isn't it only natural for someone to make wine?

"You really make wine?"

"Yeah. I really make wine."

It wasn't quite so simple. The loan officer was still ensnared in the tentacles of the octopus of capitalism, even in the People's Republic of Ithaca. After all, those ultra-liberal college professors still needed a return on their savings. So he, too, was looking for collateral. But what was different was that he wasn't a stiff-necked loan officer secretly laughing up his sleeve at someone else's dream. Instead, he was intrigued by the dream. He, too, saw the potential. He, too, felt the draw, the mystique: A winery.

Gary and Rosie got a loan for $296,000 in January 1999. Some $100,000 went for capital equipment—the stainless steel tanks, the oak barrels.

"They took a real chance on us," Rosie said. "The absolute and only reason they gave us this loan was I had that MBA." And the fact that Rosie's mother loaned them $25,000. They had collateral.

They started construction on the winery that summer. The building was due to be finished by September when Gary would crush his first grapes. Then they realized that the grapes would arrive before the federal Bureau of Alcohol, Tobacco and Firearms could inspect and approve the winery for operation. By law, they could not crush grapes until they were certified as bonded—in other words, that the wine was secured and accounted for when it came to tax purposes. They faced the prospect of grapes rotting in the building as workmen tried to finish up. In fact, the construction workers signed the receipt for the barrels when they arrived.

They got the BATF to move up the inspection. The day the BATF inspector arrived work was not finished. Exit signs still had to be posted. Windows still had to be installed. There were windowless openings where there should have been windows. The winery was not secure. The laborers rushed, nailing plywood up to cover empty windows, Rosie recalled.

It was a sunny day. A Friday. When the BATF inspection officer showed up he admired the view of the lake. Rosie suggested they take advantage of it.

"Why don't we enjoy it and do the paperwork down by the water?"

They took the BATF agent down to the state park on Cayuga Lake. There, at a picnic table, Rosie and Gary used every delaying tactic they could think of so the workmen could finish up as much as possible. They talked about how beautiful the lake view was, they talked about the business of opening the winery, they talked about how beautiful the lake view was, they talked about BATF requirements, they talked about how beautiful the lake view was.

Finally, after an hour of talking about how beautiful the lake view was, they faced the inevitable: The winery had to be inspected. They drove back. The inspector walked around and inspected the outside of the building. Then, he surprised Rosie. He didn't bother going inside. Instead, he signed what Rosie was so anxious for: certification that they were approved for business.

"He said it was the most enjoyable review he had ever done," Rosie said. "At least they got the exit signs up. But if he had come at night he would have discovered they didn't light up."

That day Gary began pressing grapes.

In those early years some of the what-ifs happened. First, MacKenzie-Childs went bankrupt in 2000. Shortly after, the Aurora Inn shut down. And then there was the one what-if no one could anticipate: 9/11.

To this day Rosie and Gary believe 9/11 was the major factor that stalled their efforts—and why it's been a harder, longer struggle than they could have anticipated in their business plan.

"On the two weekends after 9/11 we didn't have more than five customers," Rosie said. "After that, people who normally would buy a case of wine would buy only one bottle, or two."

People were frightened and cutting back on non-necessities. Wine a non-necessity? Try telling that to a true wine lover.

It was critical to stay with the business plan as much as possible, whatever the ups and downs. "Eighty percent of companies that don't follow their business plans go belly up in five years," Rosie said.

That meant staying open seven days a week as planned. It meant continuing advertising and marketing.

However, they had no choice but to cut back on projected production levels. After five years they had planned to be at 12,000 to 15,000 gallons of wine annually. The dip in the economy stalled them at 6,000 gallons.

Slowly, things began to turn around. An outside investor bought MacKenzie-Childs in 2001 and it came out of bankruptcy—although eventually a bigger store would be opened in New York City. The Aurora Inn was purchased, and from 2001 to 2003 it went through a major renovation, reopening as a high-end country inn.

Still, Long Point wasn't where it should have been according to the plan. For one thing, the loan wasn't enough.

"Pete Saltonstall once told me that you need a minimum of $500,000 to start a winery," Gary said, and that was in 1999 dollars. "I figured I could cut corners and do it for $300,000. I know how to cut corners." After all, here was a guy who didn't own anything except for a dog and an ironing board when he married Rosie. And he didn't have any debts. When it came to being frugal, he was an artist. Now, with the luxury of hindsight, he said, "I have to admit that in the end Pete was right. I really needed about $500,000." And after a decade the investment was pushing $1 million.

By 2004 sales were not where they hoped they would be after five years. "We're only doing a third of the business we planned to be doing by now," Rosie said at the end of the year. By then they had planned for the winery business to at least pay the mortgage. Instead, Gary's salary at the time went for that.

But Gary and Rosie do have their consolations. After all, Gary won the bet. And her insistence that he make award-winning whites would eventually evolve into his shift in philosophy about wine: He wanted to make the kinds of whites for which the Finger Lakes were known.

On an overcast July day a light spray of warm rain fell occasionally as Dan talked with Hans Walter-Peterson out in the Chardonnay block. "My concern is that if you drop too much fruit what you have is that the vine goes through too much canopy growth. What you get is shoot growth. I already have enough shoot growth, so much that I'm going to be coming through and cutting it off," Dan said, holding a green cluster of Cabernet Franc, small, hard berries in one hand, examining it with Hans.

Hans's lean face, crowned with short cropped hair, nodded appreciatively as Dan talked. Hans is the Cornell Cooperative Extension agent for viticulture in the Finger Lakes. He's the one who responds when grape growers have problems that spiral out of control, praying he will have the answer. Or, as in the case of Long Point, he does site visits to get better acquainted with the grape growers and their vineyards, and to offer suggestions to improve their practices. In jeans, jogging shoes, and a short-sleeved shirt, he was dressed for comfort.

"It makes more sense to wait to thin them off," Hans agreed. "Once the berry starts to change color, in most cases the vine will stop growing because it's got what it needs and there's a change in the physiology where it basically has everything it needs and shunts everything into berry development." At that point grape thinning can begin, Hans said.

Hans inspected the vines further. They had been neatly pruned and thinned. There were few weeds at the base and the naked trunk rose about two feet to where the vines branched out to right and left. Dan had already removed canopy to give the berries more sun.

"I don't think I would remove any more leaves," Hans said.

"Right. I don't think we want to sunburn the grapes," Dan said.

They also discussed pesticide application. When Gary and Joe laid out the vineyard, they planned it so it measured one acre from the end of one newly planted young vine trunk to the others in the far corners. What they didn't take into account is that the vines would grow and extended beyond the trunks. Five years later the block of mature Cabernet Franc measured more than an acre. And it made Dan, himself learning the vineyard profession, unsure of how much to spray. Should he spray fungicide according to the original measurements? Or should he include more pesticide for the additional growth, which was significant?

"You don't want to..." Hans paused to choose his words as he thought it through. "On a very small block like this it is not quite as critical. But if you're dealing with a seventeen-acre block or a twenty-one acre block or something like that, you know you get to the end... you get to the last five rows and you don't want to run out. That's going to be a royal pain in the butt."

In the end he agreed that it was better to apply more pesticide.

As much as anything, Hans was assuring Dan that his homegrown solutions were good ones. In addition to providing emergency assistance when disaster strikes in the vineyard, Hans also provides the expertise that helps Dan become more confident in working out problems on his own as they arise.

Later they walked down to the Riesling block. Cayuga Lake
stretched to the south in its glacial valley while the clouds continued
to scud overhead with an occasional light spray of raindrops.

When Dan took Hans into the first row of Rieslings, he told him,
"So right here are the 2007 plantings."

"Get out! Really?" Hans said in surprise at the beginning of the first
row, taking in their ample proportions.

The vines were now only into their third year of growth, but they
towered over the vineyard manager and cooperative extension agent.

"I'm amazed," Dan said.

And, after all, these are the Riesling that loomed increasingly large
in Gary's imagination because they could put Long Point on the map
in bigger markets. By this point so many people had talked about just
how well Riesling will grow here that I've begun to imagine a huge neon
sign arching over the Finger Lakes, something out of Toonland, blink-
ing on and off in a rainbow of colors, "Welcome to Rieslingland."

"Hah!" Hans yelped, followed by a long, hearty laugh because he
still couldn't believe what he was seeing.

It was Riesling that provided the significant shift in Gary's philosophy
about wine.

It's true that red wine had always tugged at his soul, and he had
even considered growing Cabernet Sauvignon. "At least I hope that's
what he does," Rosie told me back in 2004, because that's what she
wanted, too. After all, others were doing it in the Finger Lakes.

But Gary kept hesitating.

"They mature later than Cab Franc," he said. And that was the
problem, because Cab Franc, while it does generally very well in the
Finger Lakes, is also at risk, just not as much.

"Cab Franc needs 165 days to ripen. Let's say you have bud break
May 1. May through September is 150 days. You need those extra first
two weeks in October," he said.

One year the worst happened. He contracted with the Knapp
Winery across the lake for Cab Franc. At the end of September Gary
talked with their vineyard manager about the quality, and the manager
said they looked good. They were on track for an excellent crop—if
they could hang for two more weeks. A few days later the vineyard

manager called: A heavy frost hit, and the grapes had to be picked immediately.

If you couldn't count on Cab Franc, how could you count on Cab Sauv? It may have name recognition, but it was too risky. What he did know was that whites did very well in the Finger Lakes, especially Riesling. And if you can make world-class Riesling in the Finger Lakes, why wouldn't you?

Of course, Gary would never give up reds—nor would Rosie let him. It's too much in their DNA. But the reality of what the land could do well had changed the way he thought about winemaking. Perhaps it was something he should have appreciated when he started the winery. Anyway, by 2006 he had decided to plant Riesling and Pinot Gris, another white that does well in the Finger Lakes. The problem was his supplier miscalculated and didn't send enough Riesling plantings. Much of the effort of the season went to waste. Only in 2007 could he fully plant a block of Riesling.

A measure of his conversion was in how much he planted, three and a half acres of Riesling, twice as much as any of his other varieties.

Also, by now he had learned how important it was to take advantage of labor-saving mechanization. No more painting lines with yellow and white paint. Instead, he hired a contractor with a mechanical planter and the straight lines were laid out by a laser beam.

Dan and Hans continued inspecting the Riesling. The vines rose thick with berries and in full leaf—even more so than the Cabernet Franc they had just inspected—and the Cabernet Franc were six years old.

In reference to an earlier e-mail Hans had sent to vine growers with his assessment of how Rieslings were faring that year, Dan remarked, "Now, I saw your e-mail about how a lot of people said they have three clusters on their canes. A lot of mine have four."

Hans chuckled at a vine grower's good fortune.

"I'm pulling the fourth one off?" Dan added, seeking Hans's approval.

"These are just going…gangbusters!" Hans said.

They continued to examine the clusters.

"I would keep the crop," Hans said.

"Yeah?"

"I mean, well," and now Hans paused, considering the fecundity of nature, its possibilities, and what could be too much and what could be too little. "This is essentially a mature cane," he said pointing to one cane. "The size of it. The size of the canes. The height you're getting."

"Yeah, that's like nine feet tall," Dan said. He added that he was concerned that the site may be overly vigorous and that he was considering changing the trellis system to one that would expand the area for the vine canopy to grow.

Not yet, Hans advised. "I would wait for a couple more years and kind of see how this pans out. But, like you said, these are three-year-old vines and you can carry a decent crop on them already."

After some thought, Hans suggested, "I would probably just do *some* cluster thinning. But I wouldn't...it's always a tough thing in a vineyard like this when you have...this vine and then this vine," and Hans pointed to two vines, one more fully developed, the other less so, "so this one you would want to take more fruit off and that one you would want to leave more on."

What Dan didn't want to do is overstress the weaker vines by leaving too much crop on.

At the top of the vines the leaves were pockmarked with holes. In some instances all that was left was the delicate and fine tracery of the veins of the leaves. On one leaf a Japanese beetle nibbled away, executing its gustatory artistry.

"It's an acceptable level of damage," Hans said.

Later, as they walked to the Chardonnay block they talked about soil types. Long Point has five different soil types, and Dan considers himself lucky because other vineyards can have many times that number. "I'm just glad it's not more. It just makes it more predictable the more consistency you have."

When they reached the Chardonnay block the electric to the fence was off, and Dan pulled up on one wire with his hand while his foot pushed down the other so Hans and I could pass through.

"I'm really happy with the netting," Dan said, referring to the black synthetic netting that ran on both sides of the rows holding in vines and grape clusters. Its purpose was to discourage deer and birds, as well as to force the vines to grow upward by constraining

the sides. The netting had quarter-inch square openings in it. "It's very strong. You can't pull it apart with your hands," Dan said. Presumably the deer and birds have the same difficulty trying to get to the fruit.

"Do the vines grow through?" Hans asked.

"Yes," Dan said, pointing to where a tendril of vine had slipped through the mesh. "But to me it's a small price to pay for the protection I get."

When they reached an interior Chardonnay row, Dan said, "I'm not sure what to do first. You can see this needs weeding."

Weeds grew along a line under the trellis of vines, in sharp contrast to just how clean the Cabernet Franc had been. "But you also see that the scion has rooted in places."

What he meant was that the Chardonnay part of the vine had put out roots in an attempt to reach for the soil to transplant itself and reject the native American root system to which it had been grafted. He and Hans stared at one vine, and at the base, just above the knot of the graft union, a woody appendage some eight inches long dangled in midair seeking earth. And inevitable death.

"I know the weeds are taking nutrients from the vines," Hans said. "But the more important priority is to remove these roots. You know what will happen. And I can promise you that there is phylloxera in this soil."

By noon the site visit was over.

"It looks very good," Hans said. To be sure there were problems. But there was little in the way of disease, and the Japanese beetles munched moderately.

While extension agents such as Hans Walter-Peterson work hands-on in the field with vineyard managers and winemakers, the New York State Agricultural Experiment Station in Geneva, which sits at the top of Seneca Lake, serves as a major center for viticulture and enology research into problems confronting the winemaker and vineyardist.

In a sense, they are the court of last appeal when it comes to especially intractable problems. Funded by New York State and administered by Cornell University, the research spans the issues and concerns confronting winemakers like Gary and vineyard managers like Dan.

For example, one year Gary had a red that smelled strongly of rotten eggs—hydrogen sulfide. He treated it with copper sulphate, which usually eliminates the problem. But this time it didn't. So, he sent off a sample to the experiment station. In their analysis they advised him to add bentonite, which is a clay used for removing excess protein from wine (and is also the basis for kitty litter). Through a complex series of chemical reactions and the addition of inactive yeast, the rotten egg smell or hydrogen sulfide disappeared.

"And the wine went on to win seven medals," Gary said.

One of the research professors at the Experiment Station is Gavin Sacks, an intense young man who leavens his enthusiasm with irony. His research area is a problem that Gary and other winemakers have long had to struggle with in the Finger Lakes, an omnipresent smell stronger than the others to which the Cabernet Franc is subject. It's a chemical compound called isobutylmethoxypyrazine, whose pronunciation could serve as a mantra for putting yourself to sleep at night. Say it over and over: "ice-o-butil-methox-eee-peer-a-zine...ice-o-butil-methox-eee-peer-a-zine... "

"I just call it IBMP," said Sachs, his eyes flashing as he spoke, the professor briskly dissecting his subject for his student—in this case, me. "It makes it easier for the students."

More conventionally IBMP is called green bell pepper aroma in wines. It is of course the stuff that gives green bell peppers their distinctive herbaceous green taste. It can also ruin a good red wine such as Cabernet Franc. This is no small matter since Cab Franc is the mainstay of red *vinifera* production in the Finger Lakes. If IBMP is too strong, it overwhelms and masks the fruitiness of the wine. In fact, Gavin noted, if you took a bathtub of IBMP and poured it into Cayuga Lake, you would be able to taste it because it is so strong.

So what to do if a winemaker thinks that his wine is too herbaceous? Sacks is frank about it: The research results aren't encouraging. Once the grapes have been made into wine, there's not a lot that can be done to counteract the green bell pepper taste. While it could be stripped out with charcoal, that would also strip away desirable qualities from the wine. So far there is no known antidote once the green bell pepper taste is in wine.

What it means, then, is that the best grapes possible must be grown before they are made into wine, and that lends support to an age-old battle between the winemakers who *make* the wine, and the vineyardists who say the "wine is made on the vine." Measures to avoid IBMP in the vineyard include installing drainage tiles to draw off excess moisture from the soil because *vinifera* tends to prefer dry soils. One of the challenges of the Finger Lakes is that it rains throughout the growing season, Sacks said. Compared with the more arid growing regions of California, Italy, and southern France, the Finger Lakes is a wet growing environment, averaging thirty to fifty inches of precipitation annually. By comparison, Napa in California averages twenty-four inches but more than half of that falls in December, January, and February alone, while the rest is distributed throughout the other nine months.

Ideally, vineyardists should let Cabernet Franc mature longer on the vine, but that's not always an option when the cold weather and night frosts arrive in the early Upstate autumns. Removing leaf cover to provide more light exposure is another strategy for pushing maturity. Shoot thinning is another. These are standard practices. But still another is to avoid excessively reduced yields, in other words "undercropping," or reducing the size of the crop. Smaller crops can be achieved by removing grape clusters or by pruning vines heavily early in the season with the intention of increasing ripening in the remaining grape clusters.

"However, vine growth has been positively correlated with the presence of IBMP," Sacks said. "It sounds counterintuitive that too-small crops could be detrimental. But if you remove too much fruit you get more vine growth." By removing fruit too soon, in an effort to reduce crop size, the plants compensate for the loss of fruit by manufacturing *more* of the herbaceous green pepper compound through the entire system, which includes the grape clusters.

Meanwhile, Anna Katharine Mansfield and Becky Nelson have been trying to determine how *terroir* influences Finger Lakes Riesling. In grape growing and winemaking, *terroir* is the French concept that soil, rainfall, trellis systems, sunlight, temperature, and thinning and pruning techniques all combine to influence wine quality.

Sitting Indian-style in a summer rain, Becky was removing leaf cover.

"I forgot my raincoat," the Cornell graduate student said with an embarrassed laugh as the raindrops speckled her face, down which streaked an occasional thin rivulet.

The knees of her blue jeans had soaked through and her long blond ponytail had darkened from the rain. Fortunately for her, it was a warm rain at the Experiment Station's agricultural testing site in Lansing, New York, along the southeast side of Cayuga Lake. It's only about four miles from Ithaca and Cornell University, where Becky was earning her Master of Science degree in food science and technology. Her graduate research involved caring for six sites in the Finger Lakes region where Anna Katharine, another research professor at the Geneva Experiment Station, was conducting the *terroir* study.

"Becky has complete responsibility for the vines," Anna Katharine said, protecting herself under an umbrella from the light rain. She had driven down from Geneva to inspect progress on the project.

The *terroir* study directed from out of Geneva is part of an effort by scientists to determine if there is something special about the region. The study focuses on Riesling.

"It's pretty obvious Riesling is the white cultivar of choice," Anna Katharine said, because it's the one wine more than any from the Finger Lakes that has a reputation well beyond the region. "Our problem is we don't know what makes a Finger Lakes Riesling distinctive."

Because Australian, Rhine-Mosel-Ruwer, and Alsatian Rieslings are identifiably distinctive, Finger Lakes Riesling, if they are to be competitive internationally, would benefit from having their own identity. It's true that the Finger Lakes are a recognized AVA, or American Viticultural Area. Moreover, Seneca and Cayuga lakes have their own AVA designations. But having AVA status doesn't necessarily translate into an identity for the Riesling from the area—or the other varietals for that matter.

Becky had daily responsibility for maintaining the six sites—two on the east shore of Keuka Lake, two on the east shore of Seneca Lake, and two on the east shore of Cayuga Lake. They represent three microclimates in the Finger Lakes. Every week she visited each of the sites, and in addition to grooming the vines—removing leaf cover or making sure there are the same number of clusters on each shoot—she records rainfall, temperature, and other factors reflecting the climate.

When the grapes are harvested, wine will be made from each of the sites.

"Then we can see what difference the three microclimates of the three lakes make," Anna Katharine said. Plus, there will be soil studies. And Becky and Anna Katharine will look at different trellising systems to determine if they influence the wine.

Once wine is made in the basement of the Geneva research lab, a panel of tasters will be brought together to do blind tastings. But they won't be experts in wine.

"The people who buy those wines are not expert tasters. They are just average consumers," Anna Katharine said.

She acknowledged it won't be easy to determine the influence of *terroir*, given that in France it took generations before winemakers could understand theirs.

"But it seems like a good guess that there is something there."

Finally, the Barlettas would have some time together. And was that too much to ask on their wedding anniversary? Even if it was a blistering summer's day.

That's what Rosie thought. Because she couldn't remember the last time she and Gary celebrated the occasion. Certainly not since the winery opened. It was a time when even though they were always in each other's presence they hardly spoke to each other because they were so busy at the winery. Gary might be doing the last of the bottling. Rosie was running the tasting room and trying to keep the books straight. You had to keep the books straight. You couldn't slack off. If you did, you were dead. In her worst dreams she could imagine a BATF SWAT team surrounding the winery on a busy Sunday afternoon, helicopters swooping in overhead, men in camouflage rappelling down to the roof, while barking, growling German shepherds sniffed cowering customers in the crotch for contraband wine. Overhead, one might hear a megaphone blaring, "Come out with your hands up. And don't cook the books." Gary, bleary-eyed from working every night, would look up, insensible, saying, "A raid? A raid?" and then return to the clink of the bottling machine and say over and over, "Gotta bottle. Gotta bottle. Gotta bottle." He would keep saying it as they led him off in handcuffs, "Gotta bottle. Gotta bottle. Gotta bottle."

It wasn't that bad, she acknowledged. But there were days...

That's why the two-hour drive over to Dr. Konstantin Frank's Vinifera Wine Cellars on the west side of Keuka Lake, to the west beyond Seneca Lake, which in turn lay beyond Cayuga, was so inviting. It was escape. Or at least it was the illusion of escape because at the other end of the journey was more winery business, two new French barrels Gary had ordered. But right now they welcomed the illusion.

They took off work that day. They would each go in their own cars as far as the winery because when they returned late in the afternoon Rosie would go directly home. Gary had to clean out one of the stainless steel tanks that evening. Such was the promised conclusion to their anniversary celebration. But they would try to focus on the present. Deep down they knew that the celebration wasn't necessarily about a goal they had reached but rather the momentum of the journey they had embarked on.

Gary had gone out to the winery earlier and Rosie followed. It was the familiar journey across the high country to the west of Homer that in winter threatened treacherous whiteouts, the descent into the sheltered valley of the village of Locke, the ascent to high plateau country—the Canadian Shield that seemed to stretch forever—then down into little Genoa where you could stop at the IGA for a cup of hot coffee and a fat Italian sub if you were hungry, then on to King Ferry where the land opened out on to the broad waters of Cayuga Lake. It was part of the old routine. It was in their bones by this point. At the winery Rosie checked in briefly with the counter staff. It was only as they pulled out of the winery parking lot in Gary's pickup truck at about ten o'clock that he and Rosie felt they had finally gone beyond the boundaries of the known world and escaped over the horizon.

"It's great," Rosie said, smiling as they drove south to Ithaca to go around the southern end of the lake.

"I'm free, I'm free," Gary joked, but while there was now a sense of having left the winery behind, he also had a sense that he had gone into a freefall. He had a twinge of guilt leaving the winery behind, like a neglectful father off on a lark while his newborn fended for himself.

"Lighten up," Rosie said.

"I am," he replied. "I'm free. I'm free."

He erupted with a deep cheery laugh from his fluttering gut, and then he felt better.

They talked about what they were missing out on in their lives because of the winery: travel, time with the boys and their young families, spending time with their friends. She really missed their friends, Rosie said.

From Ithaca they turned west to Watkins Glen. It's one of the anomalies of travel in this part of the world that most through roads generally run north to south because the lie of the lakes is north-south. If you could go due west the trip might be cut to forty-five minutes. But there were these lakes, a mile to two miles wide and up to thirty-five miles long that you had no choice but to drive around. In certain place names you can detect references to a long-ago ferry, such as King Ferry. But the days when farmers ferried their teams of horses and wagons loaded with produce across the lakes were long gone. The result is that today, with the automobile, most of your travel is north-south, with occasional short jogs east-west between the lakes. This was particularly true because of Cayuga and Seneca lakes, the two largest and longest of the Finger Lakes. But it was also true of the other Finger Lakes—Owasco, Skaneateles, Keuka (the crooked lake shaped like a Y), and Canandaigua. Then there are a number of smaller lakes. Glaciation had decreed the north-south disposition, and in losing the east-west orientation you lost your bearings—travelers might not venture in and economic ventures needing easy transport bypassed the region. The result was that the necks of land between the lakes seemed forgotten by time. One could see it in villages such as Mecklenburg, where houses had weathered to a washed-out gray from lack of paint. This region is, after all, the home to the original Podunk (just northwest of Ithaca), which is little more than an empty crossroad.

And no wonder. The villages were, relatively, inaccessible, the inac-
cessibility made worse by the winters that blew in from the west and
north.

As Rosie and Gary headed west toward Watkins Glen, Gary felt
the appealing tug of the wineries that ran north up the west side of
Cayuga Lake. There was Swedish Hill. There was Lucas. There was
Cameron Hosmer's winery. Hosmer made good reds. He and Gary
shared a passion for reds.

"I wish we had time just to go tasting," Rosie said. It was one
of those realities that even though they were winemakers they never
had time to visit the competition. In fact, it was embarrassing how
little they knew about the other wineries. They were just too busy
with their own. And it was true the other way around. They rarely
received winemakers from other wineries because many of them were
also mom-and-pop operations, and they too had only enough energy
and time to go around, and that went into the winery: After all, energy and time translated into additional employees many of the small
wineries could not afford. So, like true farmers, the moms and pops
worked double-shifts. And in the isolation of your own winery you
became the standard by which you judged the rest of the world. You
became the center of the universe. Maybe it was easier on the ego that
way. Because what if you found someone making better wine than
you?

But that way of thinking was a cop out and not Gary's way. "Gary
loves competition and loves to try other wines. He says he learns a
great deal from doing it," Rosie said.

Visiting the competition, however, was unlikely to happen. It would
take too much energy that was in short supply. Gary and Rosie had to
save it for the winery. It was the energy that kept the winery going.

"Yeah, I wish we had a week," Gary said. "That would be nice. A
week." A week of no other cares but tasting other people's wines, driving around the Finger Lakes, stopping in at these little operations—
some smaller than Long Point—and staying at the little bed and
breakfasts scattered along the shores of the lakes.

But no matter how much they tried to put the winery behind them,
they kept returning to it.

"So I wonder if we should prep the ground next year for Cab Sauv?" Gary was asking himself as much as he was asking Rosie. This was when he was still weighing the risks of growing the variety.

He was reflecting on where life was taking him. He was entertaining ideas, taking advantage of this breathing space, trying to get some perspective in a land where you lose your orientation and can easily head in the wrong direction.

Although it was shoptalk, it didn't bother Rosie. "I love it when you enjoy hard work and look ahead."

"It's nice to take a break," Gary said.

"Yeah. Look how beautiful the country is," Rosie said.

But, as often happens when you escape, some other care pushed insistently into consciousness.

"Wouldn't it be nice if we could do the winery full time?"

"I would like that. Looking out at the lake all the time."

"Actually do eight hours a day at the winery, get out at six o'clock."

"Have a normal life."

They talked about the kids and the grandchildren, and the time passed as they mused on the incidentals of life that for too long lay on the periphery of their psyches. But they kept their eyes on the road ahead and what that road would inevitably lead back to: the winery.

While Cayuga Lake is the longest of the Finger Lakes, Seneca is the deepest. On its shores you find the largest collection of wineries in the region, more than thirty. There is Wagner's, one of the older wineries, which also has a microbrewery. There is Lamoreaux Landing, whose tasting room rises dramatically like a Greek temple above the vineyards overlooking the lake—you almost expect Bacchus to be cavorting playfully among the vines. Then there is Silver Thread, a small, intimate winery tucked away behind vineyards and at the edge of a wood. They use sustainable farming techniques and green energy sources. Castel Gritsch has a German restaurant as part of its operation.

After an anniversary meal of sandwiches and one glass of wine each in Watkins Glen, they continued west to Keuka Lake, through the land that time forgot, to Dr. Frank's.

Dr. Frank's is among the best known of the wineries in the Finger Lakes because of its namesake, the late Dr. Konstantin Frank. Frank probably did more than anyone to encourage the growing of *vinifera* grapes not only in the Finger Lakes but throughout the eastern United States, in a climate long deemed too challenging for them. A refugee from the Crimea after World War II, he had trained as a viticulturalist and was struck by the similarity in conditions in Crimea, which had an ancient wine grape tradition introduced by Greek colonists in classical times, and the Finger Lakes. In Crimea, winter rolled off the Russian steppe. Through viticultural practices, he was convinced that European grape varieties could be coaxed to withstand the cold northeastern winters in the United States, as well as the rot that accompanied the high humidity during the summer. He demonstrated that it could be done.

Frank died in 1977, but today his Dr. Konstantin Frank Vinifera Vineyards is particularly known for its sparkling wines made according to the Champagne method and for Riesling. The winery is now run by his grandson, Fred.

Gary and Rosie confronted reality as they drove down the country lane high atop a ridge that looked out over Keuka Lake toward a squat, red brick rambler of, say, 1950s vintage. They pulled into the parking lot. The anniversary celebration was going to give way, much as it had every year, to the business of running a winery. But, it had been fun, the drive over, the kidding, the dreaming, even the lunch of sandwiches, and although there would be the drive back, there was a feeling that the best was over.

At this time Dr. Frank's served as a central depot in the Finger Lakes for imported French oak barrels made by one prominent French cooper, Tonnellerie Remond. When a winery like Gary's ordered barrels, according to long-standing practice, they would usually be shipped to California. The winemaker at Dr. Frank's volunteered to have them shipped directly to Dr. Frank's, where area winemakers could pick them up.

This was the first time Gary had been to Dr. Frank's.

The red brick rambler, which otherwise could be someone's home, served as the tasting room. From the outside it was not so impressive compared with some of the faux châteaux built in recent years at some of the other wineries. In the distance, to the east, Keuka Lake lay in a valley between steep ridges. Behind the tasting room complex sat a big, cream-colored cinderblock warehouse.

Gary explained to the tasting room help why he had come. One went out to the warehouse—the winery proper—and brought back Morten Hallgren, the head winemaker.

He offered a wine tasting.

"Happy to," Gary said.

They followed Morten back to a private tasting room, what is called the "dungeon" at Dr. Frank's because it has no windows.

Morten pulled out three glasses. They started with a Champagne-style sparkling white because it was the Barlettas' anniversary.

"Very smooth finish," Gary said.

As they tasted they talked. "How are your grapes doing?" Gary asked, while his palate teased meaning from the aftertaste of the sparkling wine.

"I'm not really excited about the fruit out there."

"No, it's not something to be excited about. There's not a lot of good fruit," Gary agreed, thinking of his own vineyard.

"You can't leave here without trying a Riesling," Hallgren said. Riesling is one of his specialties. He pulled a bottle from a refrigerator below the tasting counter and poured.

"This is not one of our best Rieslings. This wasn't one of our best years," he said as Gary drew in the fragrance.

"No, but it has a nice nose," he said.

"That's what I liked about Morten," Rosie recalled. "He was honest about his wines. He wasn't saying all of his wines are good."

As Morten and Gary talked, Rosie listened, and she realized something for the first time that she had never fully appreciated. Here was Gary, this guy who once made wine in discarded whisky barrels in the cellar of her house while she and the kids waged war with fruit flies, being treated as an equal by another winemaker at one of the most distinguished wineries in the Finger Lakes, one whose sparkling wine was famous. The Barlettas had worked hard to establish their winery. And it was clear that here, at least in the eyes of Gary's peers, he had arrived.

Gary didn't notice he had arrived professionally. After all, to him, he was just talking shop with another winemaker. It was second nature for a winemaker.

It only got better. Morten invited them back to the warehouse to continue tasting from the barrels.

First they went upstairs to where the whites were stored.

"This is just a beautiful Chardonnay," Morten said of the 2002 as he withdrew some with a wine thief. "There's not a lot of oak. It's ageworthy. It has longevity."

"Very nice. How often do you stir the lees?"

"Weekly. Then I back off and do it every couple of weeks."

Next they went downstairs and tried the young reds.

"It was like being asked to have tea with the Pope," Rosie recalled.

Gary and Morten later went out to load the two barrels into the back of the pickup. They picked up the first barrel and on the count of three heaved it up and over the tailgate. They turned it upright. Then they did the second barrel.

Later, as Gary and Rosie returned to Long Point that late summer afternoon, she looked back through the rear window of the truck at the new French barrels sitting squat and imperious—the white oak staves shining brightly in the sun. And for the first time she could appreciate them in a new light.

On a wilting summer's day in Ithaca, the heat had built up in the deep valley between the ridges so it was hard to believe it was ever winter here, a deep, bone-chilling winter that, like its seasonal opposite summer, gets trapped in the valley. Russ Nalley walked across an asphalt parking lot blistering in the sun and into one of the major wine retailers in the area. He found the racks dedicated to New York State wines and stopped at the one holding Long Point bottles.

"I like it at the end. That sets it off for the consumer. It gets good visibility," said Gary's marketing manager.

With generous, good-humored proportions, Russ was dressed in a loud, short-sleeved floral print shirt more suitable for Miami Beach. But it was part of his sales image—the Long Point logo ran above his shirt pocket. When Russ was pleased, I observed, his ample push broom of a moustache curled up happily at the corners. At forty-three, he was a hail-fellow-well-met type. For example, when Gary first introduced us, Russ quipped: "Maybe I could get naked with a couple of blond babes in the wine tank?" and his moustache pushed up at the ends.

Gary looked at him skeptically.

Russ looked at the racks in the store, some of which were nearly empty. People were buying Long Point. "That's what I like to see."

Despite the cheerful moustache, Russ had a tough day of sales ahead of him. And in the end he would win some, lose some.

When Gary and Rosie opened Long Point, nothing could prepare them for the realities of marketing. As Gary made his wine, the cardboard cases began to accumulate, building one atop the other in the winery. Case by case, the structure rose toward the winery ceiling like a tower to Gary's hubris, announcing to anyone who took the time to look at it: You can make all the wine you want. But you've also got to sell it.

At times, Gary and Rosie felt they spent more time selling their wine than making it.

The most important means for marketing wine remains, of course, the tasting room. But important in their own way are the onsite special events, such as the Wine and Herb Festival, the offsite special events, such as the Finger Lakes Wine Festival in Watkins Glen, and, finally, the liquor stores and restaurants carrying the Long Point line. Without national distribution because they were so small and new, it was all up to Gary and Rosie in the early days.

At first, in his innocence, Gary drove around to liquor stores and restaurants in the area, selling his wine door-to-door.

"It was a disaster," Rosie said. Not so much because Gary is not a salesman but because that's just not the way to present the vintage: The little old winemaker shows up in his rusted-out Toyota pickup with a case in his arms trying to peddle wine to liquor stores. It was only a half-step above a guy selling frozen steaks of dubious origin out of the trunk of a car. And in the wine business, an important part of the equation is presentation. Add to this that Gary was selling his wine while working a full-time job and running the winery.

Their first liquor store and restaurant accounts were almost still-born, like a vintage gone bad. As Rosie recalls, with a touch of exaggeration because it is all too funny now, "I almost went to jail because I didn't have a license to distribute."

Their first wines were ready in fall 2000 and accounts had been solicited from Plaza Liquors in Cortland and the King Ferry Hotel restaurant in King Ferry, the latter not far from Long Point Winery. These were safe bets. Rosie and Gary were well known and well liked by the hospital crowd so there was, hopefully, a built-in customer base in Cortland. That explained the Plaza. The proximity of King Ferry Hotel to the winery gave the wine a local cachet it shared with nearby King Ferry Winery. So, one Friday afternoon Gary dropped off two cases at Plaza and a case at the hotel.

That evening Rosie received a call from the King Ferry Hotel.

"Can you give us the registration number for your wholesale license?"

"I'll have to find it."

She paged through the assortment of licenses she stuffed away in a manila file but couldn't find it. She called back.

"What number? What license was that?"

That's when she discovered that among the different licenses she had to have—a retail license from the state Liquor Authority, one from the then federal Bureau of Alcohol, Tobacco and Firearms because they were a bonded winery, as well as a certificate to collect state sales tax, and a license from the state's Department of Agriculture and Markets to permit wine tastings on the premises—they also needed a wholesale license.

Their retail license to operate as a winery didn't cover wholesale. Also, they had to advertise their prices thirty days in advance before they could sell wholesale.

The state liquor authority was closed for the weekend so Rosie didn't know what to do. But she discovered that the fine for selling wine without a wholesale license is $30,000.

That would sink them.

"You've got to be kidding me! People are buying our wines and we have to take it away from them?" Gary said when Rosie told him.

The next morning a sheepish Gary drove over to Plaza Liquors and asked for his wine back. The conversation went like this:

"What's wrong with it?"

"Nothing's wrong with it."

"Something's got to be wrong with it."

He explained.

Then he drove out to King Ferry Hotel. He arrived at lunchtime. As he walked into the dining room, he saw a couple of women drinking a bottle of his wine—the Cambrie, his first commercial vintage. It was probably the most difficult situation a winemaker ever had to confront: To tell people they could not drink his wine.

What do I do? he thought. Do I stop them from drinking?

Meanwhile, he heard one of the women say to the waitress, "We would like another bottle of the wine."

He went up to the bartender to explain while another bottle was delivered to the table.

"They can't drink that bottle of wine," Gary said, after he introduced himself as the winemaker at Long Point.

The bartender looked at him skeptically: Was this guy crazy?

"What do you mean they shouldn't be drinking it? What's wrong with it?"

"Nothing's wrong with it. I need to recollect all the wine I dropped off."

"You're kidding."

"No. I didn't know we needed a separate license to sell wholesale."

"I didn't either. So what do I do about the bottle of wine on the table?"

"See if they'll take a pitcher of beer," Gary said gamely.

The bartender walked over to the couple and, with many apologies, said she couldn't sell them the bottle of wine. Gary watched the faces of wine drinkers who were enjoying his wine—the first vintage of his winery, the first born of his deepest heart's desire, *his* wine—turn confused and then shocked as the bartender explained that there was nothing wrong with the wine, but that there was some kind of licensing problem. When the bartender nodded at Gary and the customers looked at him, he wanted to crawl into an empty wine barrel and pull the bung behind him. Instead, he smiled politely at the customers and felt like a silly fool, which is something Gary Barletta as a matter of principle normally wouldn't feel for anyone. Today was different because the episode cut to the heart of what he believed about himself: He was a winemaker. And now he was telling people not to drink his wine. So, he was a fool, and he confiscated the remaining case and made a hasty retreat.

That afternoon one of the women from the restaurant came into the winery. Rosie was at the wine-tasting counter. The woman explained that a strange man with a beard had come into the King Ferry Hotel restaurant and confiscated her bottle of wine.

"Yeah, I know. That was my husband."

Then Gary walked in.

"You're the one who took the bottle of wine off the table. So why did you do it?"

"We didn't know we needed a wholesale license," Gary said.

"She was not offended," Rosie said later. "She was very down to earth and understood. We offered our apologies." And Rosie gave her a bottle of wine.

"She also left here buying more wine," Rosie said.

Monday morning Rosie called the state liquor board to explain. "I'm sorry. Please don't fine me $30,000. We're new at this. I didn't understand the rules. My mother always told me to tell the truth," she said.

"You did what?" the lady at the other end of the line said. "Your husband did what?" And she burst out laughing. "Is that all you did? Look, we've got bigger fish to fry."

She told Rosie not to worry about it.

The next month it turned out that they posted the prices on the wrong day. Rosie made another tearful call. And so it happened during the course of the first few months as Rosie learned the intricacies of wholesaling law that she made distraught calls after she figured out she had broken the law and feared a $30,000 fine or going to jail.

Finally, after five months, the lady at the state liquor board said, "Look. Don't call me. If you do something wrong, I'll call you."

The challenge facing Russ that day at the wine retailer in Ithaca was that Long Point had run out of Chardonnay and the next vintage would not be bottled for another month. Gary uses a portable bottler who brings in a bottling machine in a box trailer to service Finger Lakes wineries that don't want to invest in the capital expense of their own bottling line. But the bottler was booked up until the end of the month and Gary was out of Chardonnay now.

Russ's concern was that he didn't want to lose space for the Chardonnay at the wine store as well as at a nearby Ithaca restaurant he was also visiting that day. He would try to substitute Gary's Sauvignon Blanc, as well as a dry Riesling at the restaurant, until the Chardonnay was bottled. If he was successful, it might also be a way to get the store and restaurant to pick up another varietal. At least that was Russ's way of looking on the bright side. Russ waved down Alice Peters, the assistant manager, who had advised me on the market for native varietals. She was exiting a small office at the front of the store.

"I have something I think you might like," Russ said. He towered over Alice, like Falstaff, even though he is not tall. Alice was a small, warm brunette with an agreeable, cheerful smile.

At that moment, Dana Malley, the store's general manager and the principal wine buyer, walked by. Russ caught his attention. "Hey, Dana. I was just telling Alice, I have something you might like. We just released it. A Sauvignon Blanc. It's out in the car."

As the store's main wine buyer, Dana is also its main wine taster. Young and affable, Dana's short curly hair, parted in the middle, made him look more like a college kid, hardly the rumpled, grizzled gray beard of a professional wine taster with many years of experience that one might expect.

"Well, I was just going on lunch, but…," Alice said.

"Then after lunch?" Russ asked, the moustache twitching agreeably.

She nodded. "That's fine." Dana agreed.

"How about one?" Russ said.

"See you then."

In the meantime Russ dropped off two cases on order at the receiving door, where an employee checked them in. An hour later Russ was in the main office at the back of the store. The raised office floor looked out through a large window on to the store floor. From there you could watch customers. Russ took the chilled Sauvignon Blanc out of the portable cooler and opened it, pouring it into two glasses offered by Dana.

Dana and Alice took their long sniffs of wine and tasted.

"It's more tropical fruit than anything. I get…I get a lot of lime in this, more than anything," Dana said.

"Okay," Russ said.

"It could use a little more acid, actually," Dana said.

"Okay," Russ said, his voice rising as he sensed the direction the sale was taking.

"Yeah, I would go with the acid. It's a little flat on the palate," Alice said.

More silence. Dana and Alice reflected on how the taste lingered. Alice cleared her throat to speak when Dana said, affability gone, "Let me put it this way. If I were a New Zealand Sauvignon Blanc drinker and I bought a bottle of that, I wouldn't...I would have a little difficulty." And now you could tell he was picking his terms carefully. "And right now that's what you're going up against, New Zealand definitely."

Russ's voice descended now, deflated, but he would make one last try.

"This was...The way I've been approaching this is they are...It is user-friendly for those just getting into Sauv Blanc."

"Yeah," Dana said.

"But I just wanted you guys to try it," Russ said.

"Yeah. It's clearly a well-made wine. These's no question about it," Dana said. "It's just that for me it just doesn't have that Sauvignon Blanc character I look forward to."

"Okay. I understand," Russ said, his voice going up another octave with the magnanimity of defeat as his moustache twitched pleasantly.

You lose some.

Getting restaurants to carry the Long Point label was the toughest part. Because at restaurants as much effort goes into preparing the wine list as the menu. Restaurants don't like to have to reprint wine lists. So they are conservative about the wines they will serve, and a little-known startup winery such as Long Point didn't appear to be a promising bet, especially in central New York where you have so many small wineries to choose from.

One of their first restaurant accounts was Rosalie's in the village of Skaneateles (pronounced "Skinny-Atlas"—imagine Atlas without the muscles), a well-to-do waterfront community on the Finger Lake of the same name about forty-five minutes from the winery. Gary and

Rosie got their entrée because Gary had known the maître d' since his amateur winemaking days.

"I was never so nervous," Rosie said, recalling the sunny afternoon in early spring when they tried to persuade Rosalie's general manager, Steve Ansteth, and the bar manager, Barry Wright, to carry their wines.

They brought six wines for tasting. Gary poured the first. As Rosie recalled, they sniffed, then tasted.

They said nothing.

"I'm usually pretty comfortable about public presentations. But that day I could feel my heart pounding," Rosie said.

Gary poured another one. His audience sniffed, tasted, said nothing.

"When they didn't say anything that's when I started to worry," Rosie said.

Then came the third wine.

Silence.

They tasted the six wines, followed by the long silences.

Gary and Rosie were certain they had flopped.

But then, as Rosie recalled, Barry said, "You're a very good winemaker, Gary. What are you doing making wine in the Finger Lakes?" It was the way he said it, as if, "You should be off in Napa Valley or Bordeaux, using your talents for the greater good of mankind." Steve Ansteth echoed the same thoughts.

Rosalie's picked up two of the wines and has carried them ever since.

"It's not easy," Rosie said. "Without a marketing staff, without a distributor, it's hard to get your foot in the door."

Eventually, they hired a professional salesperson, someone who had sold hair-care products, with full salary and benefits—no easy decision given the tight cash flow. After all, they had to pay the mortgage. But even then liquor stores and restaurants kept turning them down. Eventually they had to let the salesperson go.

There were times when they did tastings and no one showed up to taste. One rainy autumn evening Rosie drove up to Auburn to do a wine tasting at a liquor store. This was after she had worked her day job. She was tired, and it was cold and wet and the kind of weather that kept people at home in their burrows, thinking about moving to Arizona. She placed her wines on a table at the liquor store and waited. And waited. And waited. No one showed up to taste.

And the recitative to any wine tasting that she knew so well—"It has just a hint of blackberry...," echoed mockingly in her mind as she drove back home over the winding, rain-slick roads in the dark.

When is enough enough? she could only ponder.

But in time Long Point did pick up liquor stores and restaurants, as Rosie and Gary did the marketing themselves. Then, in 2006, they hired Russ, who had experience in beer marketing but prefers drinking wine. Today, Long Point distributes to more than sixty-five liquor stores and restaurants in Upstate New York. They go as far east as Albany and as far west as Buffalo. Liquor stores generally sell the line because customers who have been out to the winery ask for it. And that is still the best way for a small winery to sell wine. Customers who like what they taste at the winery spread the news at wine and liquor stores, who then pick up the label.

Now, 22 percent of the winery's sales come from liquor stores and restaurants.

After the wine retailer, Russ dropped off a case of wine in the kitchen of the Ithaca restaurant. He had also made arrangements for a tasting to temporarily replace the Chardonnay with the Sauvignon Blanc or dry Riesling. After the delivery he returned to his minivan and retrieved the cooler bag with the chilled Riesling and Sauvignon Blanc. Even though it was a longer way around by not going through the kitchen entrance, he walked to the front of the restaurant and in the main entrance. "I don't like to get in the way of the kitchen staff," he said, but I couldn't help but wonder if front-door entrances make a better impression. You don't want to be mistaken for the kitchen help. At the entrance to the dining room a board announced the luncheon specials: onion fries, Tuscan bean and mushroom soup, and a steak wrap with olives, red pepper, and provolone.

Jennifer Coyne, the assistant food and beverage manager, met Russ at the bar. She was dressed in a dark suit, and her face was framed by carefully coiffed blond tresses, very formal, managerial. Yet, she couldn't conceal a look of preoccupation. It was still lunchtime, and like the conductor of a symphony Jennifer looked more focused on orchestrating a multitude of details. Now she had to deal with this guy who wanted to sell wine.

Russ explained the problem with the Chardonnay, how it wouldn't be bottled for another month.

"We have a couple of options to sort of fill the spot until then, Riesling and Sauvignon Blanc," he said. "Sauvignon Blanc, all dry white, all stainless steel, um...it's..."

"I would love to have the Sauvignon Blanc," Jennifer said.

"Okay?"

"Sure."

Russ pulled the cork and poured into a glass she had taken from the bar.

"Especially with your Friday night fish fry, it would go real well," he said. "That was released about a week-and-a-half ago, and people just love it. Generally I'm not a Sauvignon Blanc person but I do like that. I've had a couple of bottles of that already."

"I really like that," Jennifer said, and for a moment the preoccupation with the lunch crowd passed.

"Good."

"Very good," she said.

Russ's hopes were raised.

He now pulled the cork on the Riesling.

"How is it going to be comparable to Thirsty Owl?" Jennifer asked, referring to another Finger Lakes Riesling on the restaurant's wine list.

Russ poured as he spoke, "It's going to be a little lighter, a little crisper."

He explained how it would go well with foods, "even with salmon salad, lobster salad," because it was spicy.

But Jennifer didn't go for it. The preoccupation had returned to her expression. Her head shook back and forth, slowly.

"You know your customers better than I do," Russ said, his voice going up.

"Right."

"I just wanted to present a couple of options to you until we get the Chardonnay bottled," he said.

"I'll take the Sauvignon Blanc."

"Very good," he said firmly, as if firmness amounted to a signature on a contract. His moustache twitched happily. "I'll get that down here tomorrow."

"Beautiful," she said.

You win some.

Some years are good in the vineyard. Such as when Hans visited Dan. But other years you are reminded of just how much of a gamble you've undertaken when even what is supposed to be beneficial can turn the vineyard into a disaster. There was the summer, for example, when the "noble" rot went wild—and there was nothing noble about it.

It had been a rainy summer, and on a Saturday in August I stopped by Long Point. Gary was hosing out a garbage can. I doubt the Baron de Rothschild was ever so fortunate.

"Hey, you finally found me," he said. We had been ships passing in the night for the last two weeks. "Let me show you something."

I followed him through the lab and out the back door to a trash dumpster. He opened the lid and pulled out a cluster of green Chardonnay. Except that 30 percent of them had a yellowish brown rot, like yellow curds. Another cluster looked to be 50 percent rot. Clearly, Joe was doing some heavy trimming.

"The rain's killing us," Gary said.

Down in the Chardonnay I found Joe, and he looked like an automaton manipulated by a large, unseen force, some software of the vine sending out instructions as he rocked from one foot to the other and his left arm and hand shot out to rake the sides of the grapevines, his gloved fingers grasping at the leaves, ripping them from the leafy canopy to reveal the clusters of hard, light green Chardonnay grapes. His back was wet with perspiration. He wore a motorcycle tee-shirt that said "Triumph" on it (he owns a vintage Triumph motorcycle). The leaves fell at his feet.

Through earphones he listened to a popular song on the radio. Joe moved to his own choreography, removing leaves, under a sky that stretched all the way to the horizon, unbroken by clouds. The vines were in full leaf and the rows walked in single file to the horizon at the top of the hill, where they dropped off, like walking the plank. You couldn't see the other side and it was here that the eye, contained as it was by the green wall of leaves in front and in back of you, met the sky. It could've been confining, and yet it was comforting, too.

It was important at Long Point that Joe removed leaves because of the way Gary had to run the Chardonnay east to west to avoid erosion. Because of the lay of the Finger Lakes, most vineyards taking advantage of the way the slopes parallel the lakes get the advantage of sun on the east side of the vines in the morning, and on the west side in the afternoon. With Gary's Chardonnay block there is a slight swale that interrupts the usual north-south orientation. So, Joe left more leaves on the south face to protect the grapes, which could fry during a lengthy bout of hot weather. But that wasn't the problem now.

As he continued to strip leaves, he pointed out an occasional grape cluster with the yellowish brown taint to it. "Bunch rot. Too much rain." Bunch rot is another name for noble rot, and the grapes were covered with the greasy, mucous-like substance.

Because of rain Joe couldn't spray the plants with fungicide, and right now they badly needed either sunlight or spraying, and preferably both.

Afflictions of the vine are hardly new. There is an old church prayer from the mid-1500s that a priest would invoke to warn off assorted plagues from visiting their scourges on the grapevines:

Trusting in the divine mercy...I summon, and by the Holy Cross, armed with the shield of faith, I command and I conjure, a first, a second and a third time all flies...and all other maggots hurtful to the fruit of the vines, to cease immediately their ravaging, eating, destroying, and annihilating of the branches, buds, and fruits, to cease to have this power henceforward, and to withdraw into the remotest places of the forests so that they can

no longer harm the vines of the faithful...and if, by the coun-
sel of Satan, they refuse to obey these injunctions and continue
their devastations...I curse and hurl sentence of malediction and
anathema.

There were other methods as well for seeking divine protection in
the vineyard. One ancient Greek ritual required ripping a white rooster
in half. Two men each took a bloody half and ran around the vineyard
in opposite directions. At the location where they met they buried the
two halves. Thus they had invoked Dionysus's protection.

That's what Long Point and the other wineries in the region needed
at the moment—some divine protection.

Summer bunch rot, the specific fungus afflicting Long Point's vines,
is caused by the botrytis fungus and is just one of a host of vine diseases that the vineyardist has to deal with. Among the more widely
known are downy mildew, powdery mildew, leaf rot, and black spot.
Then there are pests, especially the notorious phylloxera.

Bunch rot is one of the most common infections in the Finger Lakes.
The infection thrives in cool, humid weather. That's why the Finger
Lakes region is ideal for the disease. It usually appears in August as
the grapes ripen. French hybrids and *vinifera* are especially vulnerable.
The fungus can attack ripe grapes directly. Skin wounds on the grape
caused by the grape berry moth, birds, and hail are particularly susceptible to the fungus. Once a grape is infected, the rot spreads rapidly
through the rest of the cluster.

That's the malevolent side to botrytis. But there is also a beneficial
side. If it is restrained by midday sun it can add some flavor to wines.
That's when it is called "noble rot." The rot causes the grape to shrivel
and concentrate sugar and flavor. It is a necessity for the sweet Hun-
garian dessert wine Tokay. Riesling grapes also benefit from it.

The problem is you can never get rid of the fungus because it spends
the winters in debris on the ground, as well as in the vine. In the spring
spores spread either by wind or in the splash of raindrops to newly
emerging leaves.

Besides fungal diseases such as summer bunch rot, there are bac-
terial diseases such as crown gall, in which a fleshy white growth
like a callus or tumor grows on the vine early in the season. Later in

the summer it turns brown, and eventually dry and corky in the fall. Crown galls, too, can affect the quality of the grapes.

But perhaps the most famous plague of the vine is not a disease. It is the bug phylloxera that Hans guaranteed to Dan was in the soil at Long Point. Phylloxera is an aphid-like insect about one millimeter long—in other words, just visible to the eye—that sucks the nutrients from the roots of the vines. Slowly, the vines wither and die. Because the parasite is native to the eastern United States, native vines are generally immune.

In the 1860s cuttings from native American vines brought to France introduced the phylloxera and it spread rapidly among *vinifera*, first in that country and then elsewhere in Europe. Within twenty years 90 percent, or some 6.2 million acres, of French vineyards had been destroyed by the parasite. French winemaking was saved only when the French *vinifera* were grafted on to disease-resistant American rootstock.

I saw Joe a few days later, and the bunch rot had now abated on its own. The sky was milky in color and humid, and the sun shone, which undoubtedly helped with the abatement. Joe took his rocking sideways walk along the arbor and his arm and hand extended like a mechanical rake to rip at a few leaves that fell at his feet. He did it by feel, ripping off one or two more, one or two less.

Then Joe paused as he snipped a grape cluster that looked perfect but for one grape that had turned yellowish brown—the fungus. He dropped the entire cluster into the white bucket on his arm. Later, back at the wheelbarrow, he dumped the bucket with its clusters. It could have been a picture for a gourmet or wine magazine, the newly picked clusters, the abundance of nature, except that they all had signs of rot.

Joe guessed that overall 3 to 5 percent of the crop was affected. As long as it didn't get much worse he could live with it because he would have to prune clusters anyway to concentrate nutrients in the best grapes. Fortunately, there was no evidence of the other diseases.

His hand reached out for the face of the canopy and raked at the leaves, again. The hair falling over his brow was damp with sweat.

Between the rich green arbors, isolated from the rest of the world, the heat was deafening.

The experiments at Geneva to identify IBMP—the green bell pepper flavor—also reveal much about tasting science and tasting art. Gavin Sacks gave me a demonstration one day of just how complex tastes can get.

"It begins with the nose, it ends with the nose," he said.

The test was simple and uses a convection oven, he explained. First, you insert a needle-like syringe filled with your sample into the tiny hole of an injector plug, then push down the plunger like you would inject a patient. Unseen, the sample from the wine flows into a column-like container in the oven.

"It's really just a very expensive convection oven you could cook a turkey or pizza in. A tasty one at that, although on the small side," Gavin said.

After turning on the oven, and as the temperature rises, aroma compounds begin to emerge—and change. Usually the first is any trace amounts of hydrogen sulfide—the rotten-egg smell—because it has a low boiling point. Others can include the smell of root beer, mushrooms, cherries, watermelon, bubble gum, and vanilla.

"Vanilla is at the high end. Its boiling point is higher because it's relatively nonvolatile compared to the others."

There are anywhere from fifty to a hundred chemical compounds that we can readily smell in wine because they are volatile, meaning they give their odors away. These compounds are among the ten thousand detectable by state-of-the-art equipment in what is called the head space just above the liquid surface of wine in a glass.

The many tastes or aromas explain why, after sipping wine, sophisticated enophiles say they can detect retronasally—or in the air passage between nose and palate—such flavors as vanilla, tobacco, leather, plum, raspberry, citrus, and others one finds described on the tasting sheets at wineries. The chemical compounds that make up the

flavors exist in wine in varying amounts. It also explains why the uninitiated sometimes read the lists and wonder if vanilla, plum, or raspberry have been added to the wine. They haven't. But such descrip-
tions aren't just fancy poetry made up by the winemaker. There is a
basis in chemistry that the astute winemaker can detect through his
nose and palate. Wine grapes, then, are a kind of chameleon, forever
offering different flavors according to varietal, *terroir,* and winemaking method, among just some of the many complex factors.

In 1990 the Department of Viticulture and Enology at the University
of California, Davis, issued a wine aroma wheel developed by one of
their own, Ann Noble. Its purpose is to encourage uniform descriptive
criteria. The wheel breaks wine down into twelve aroma groups, such
as "herbaceous or vegetative," "caramel," and "chemical." The twelve
categories are further broken into twenty-seven subgroups with such
characterizations as "fresh," "dried," and "petroleum." These categories are finally divided into eighty-eight different aromas, among them,
"blackberry," "tobacco," and "butterscotch." The decidedly more unusual include "sauerkraut," "artichoke," and "soy sauce." Then there
is "leesy," which means the aroma of the lees. This aroma can arise
when the dead yeast cells from the fermentation process have not been
removed (racked) or only inadequately removed.

Petroleum has its own category. Within it are four aromas: tar, plastic, kerosene, and diesel. Apparently gasoline didn't make the cut.

Perhaps the most peculiar is "wet dog," which is a result of micro-
bial spoilage, according to Sacks.

The aroma compounds are central to enjoying fine wine—in other
words, trying to tease meaning from them. But one either has a natural
palate or an average palate that requires time to learn to identify aromas. In fact, the latter often make better wine tasters in Sacks's view:
"People who are highly sensitive to aroma compounds are terrible
at describing wine in terms that others can use, since they are usually overwhelmed by one component of the wine. My experience has
been that people of average sensitivity to odors are usually the best at
describing wine. The difference between 'good' and 'bad' is generally
a matter of practice and experience. Individuals who have practiced
describing the flavors they are experiencing are better at the task than
those who have not."

So, there was hope for me. And for many, every advance in the knowledge of wine aromas is hard earned.

For example, I recall the time Gary said to me, "Here. Try this." He directed me to fill my wine glass from a stainless steel sixty-gallon tank holding a red wine he didn't identify.

I leaned over, placed my glass under the cock, and turned. I filled a quarter of the glass and lifted the glass to my nose.

"What kind of varietal is it?" Gary asked, testing me.

The rim of the glass at my nose, I closed my eyes and inhaled. I drew in slowly from the head space. What is it? I told myself to use my imagination. Lately I had been telling myself that. Don't be too cautious. And use your imagination. And I had been having some surprising results. Blackberry came to mind. That was an easy one. And, yes, some tobacco. The slightly aromatic hint of tobacco suggested to me that this was not a more subdued wine, say a subtle Merlot.

I tasted. I lolled the wine around in my mouth, drawing air over my tongue so my retronasal passages picked up the nose from the opposite direction—the retronasal air passages are where we get most of our tastes from and, in a way, it's like smelling backwards. Yes, the tobacco. And a hint of saddle leather?

"There is something about this that is too robust for a Merlot," I said. In my imagination the wine had a plebian, workmanlike designation—like that of a blacksmith, lots of leather and sweat and heated iron. "My inclination is to say that it's a Cabernet."

"You're right. It's a Cabernet. Which one?"

Of course, there was very little of what I described that would probably find a place on the Davis tasting wheel. But it was a beginning.

I took another sip. Very robust, but Gary likes to make full-bodied wines. Again, I think of a blacksmith hammering away. There is strength to it, raw muscularity.

"It is so robust I think it has to be a Cabernet Franc."

"You're right."

And he grinned. The novice was learning.

"You know. That's the first time I've been able to pick out a varietal," I said.

"Congratulations." He chinked my glass with a congratulatory toast.

"I still find it overwhelming. Trying to pick out the subtle differences."

"It's a matter of time. Just stay with it."

"But I wonder sometimes how much these tastes we attribute to wines are real, and how much they are imagined? You know. The power of suggestion. You tell me a wine tastes like something and when you tell me only then can I taste it."

"Well, you can tell when a wine doesn't taste like something," Gary said. "But it is hard sometimes. I remember I had a wine I was having problems with, and I sent it off to be analyzed. When the report came back, the taster said it tasted like mouse piss. I said 'Come on. How can someone know what mouse piss tastes like?'" He laughs now, recalling the incident, "But that gave me an idea for a label." Mischief arose in him, and Gary grinned. He suggested a crude label of a mouse pissing. Kind of like the cheap French table wine gussied up and marketed on Valentine's Day as "Old Fart." Then there is its companion, a red, called "Old Fart's Wife."

We returned to discussing the Cabernet Franc.

"To me there was something industrial about it that I couldn't put my finger on," I said.

"Yeah. You're right. I was thinking maybe like road tar. It was like road tar."

"Yeah. Road tar. I could go with that." It fit. And two wine drinkers agreed. Was this the truth in wine? But then I wondered, how does Gary know what road tar tastes like? For that matter, how do I? And how much of this is just the pretty poetry of an enophile's deepest longings?

Undoubtedly, some. As Anna Katharine Mansfield from the Geneva Experiment Station told me, "It's been demonstrated that people are very susceptible to tasting suggestions."

Yet, there is no doubt that there is a tasting science, as Gavin noted, because *vinifera* grapes are composed of so many tasting compounds that compete for the attention of the nose and the palate. Tasting the Cabernet Franc was one hard-earned if imperfect victory in learning how to taste.

Another time, at home, I tasted one of Gary's wines—a white. I let my imagination run wild. I closed my eyes, inhaled the head space, then drank, letting the wine lie on my palate. And it was startling what popped into my mind: Pineapple, I thought. Definitely pineapple.

But there was something else there. Some berry, perhaps? I thought about it and sipped some more. Some fruit. Apricot? Prune? Plum?... Prune? Plum? Yes, one of those two.

Later I went online to the Long Point website because I was curious. How did Gary describe it? I found the wine. I read his wine notes: "Plum with a hint a pineapple."

At first I was exhilarated. I was close. But then I thought, that's not right. That's not a hint of pineapple. That *is* pineapple. Gary, you're wrong. It's pineapple with a hint of plum or prune. But prune probably wasn't something you wanted to put in a wine description.

Later I told him: "You got it wrong, Gary. It has strong pineapple with a hint of plum."

We laughed at the apprentice, the amateur, the mere understudy, challenging the master. But then Gary added grumpily, nervous that maybe I had detected something he hadn't, "You never know..."

There could be explanations, of course. Flavors can change when wine ages in the bottle, pineapple perhaps asserting itself. And there is the final trump card in tasting: Everyone's palate is unique—similar but nonetheless unique. You say plum. I say pineapple.

By this point, I was on a tear. Not long after I was tasting at one of the Finger Lakes wineries, and no less than the winemaker was pouring. The wines were good. But then he poured a red. I tasted and burst out laughing.

"What?" he asked.

"No," I said, musing absentmindedly, trying to deflect the conversation.

"No, what?"

"Nah...it's not important."

"No, I want to know."

"Well, okay," I started. "It's a good wine." And it was. "But I've been learning to trust my first reactions. And to me...well, to me..."

"What?" he insisted.

"To me it tasted like meatballs."

The winemaker looked crestfallen.

"Well, that's why I let my wife write the tasting notes," he said.

"But it is a good wine," I tried to reassure him.

He didn't look like he believed me.

Outside the garage door of the winery, the fields had turned a bleached yellow from the August sun.

"Has anybody ever figured out how to open one of these bags without ripping it?" Gary asked, as he tore open the top of a fifty-pound brown bag of Domino Sugar, manhandled it into his arms as if cradling an oversized baby, and began pouring the contents into a blue plastic tub more suitable for washing your laundry in if you lived in a developing country. He poured about half the bag into the tub. The sugar rose in a white mound.

He put the bag down beside the tub, took up the hose attached to the hot water tank, and turned it on. The hot water poured out in a moderate silver stream. Gary placed the hose in the blue tub and began to fill it.

In some ways making sugar water symbolizes just how low he's had to stoop, because he only wants to make fine dry wines. And now he was making the sweet red wine designed for wine drinkers who haven't developed the taste yet for dry wines. A lot of wineries were doing it now. And for Gary, Moon Puppy is, discouragingly, his biggest seller.

"Moon Puppy, Moon Doggie, Moon Pooch, call it whatever you want. It's what people want to drink," he said.

Moon Puppy was strictly a marketing decision. Rosie pushed Gary to make the sweet wine. She got the name *Moon Puppy* from a Crayola crayon contest. Moon Puppy had been suggested as a name for a crimson color. "Never will I call a wine Moon Puppy," Gary protested, when she first told him the name she had picked out. He would continue to resist, she said, because to him such sweet wines really are not what wine is about.

Moon Puppy was also something of an accident. In 2003 Gary received a shipment of New York–grown Cabernet Franc. They came in under mature—way under mature. Gary had contracted the year before for the grapes. When they arrived, he was stuck with them.

Their sugar content was seventeen Brix, well below optimum. The result was that they were highly astringent, tart, acidic, thin, with the disagreeable green bell pepper taste that can haunt Cabernet Franc.

"I don't think I can do anything with these," he told Rosie. He would have to blend them with ripe grapes to make the wine more palatable and it would still be bad wine.

But Rosie had other plans. Because she knew that for marketing purposes they needed a sweet red wine. It was a sensitive issue for Gary.

"Why don't you make a sweet wine out of them?" she said.

"We don't talk that way around here," he said.

"I'm not working at the winery anymore. And I want my money back," she countered, and she had him, although it's doubtful she would have followed through. But she left him an out. "Just crush them and put them up for the year. What's it going to hurt? You can dump it next year if you can't do anything with it."

He conceded the point and made the wine.

And a year later the Cabernet Franc was still too astringent.

"I'm going to dump it."

But Rosie knew him too well.

"No, you're not," Rosie said. "You're a good winemaker. I know you can do something with it."

She had been planning on the Moon Puppy line for some time. She knew they had to do it based on the experience of other wineries in the area. Fulkerson's Winery in the Finger Lakes produces six thousand cases of their Red Zeppelin and sells out every year. King Ferry Winery has their sweet wine. So does the Knapp Winery across the lake. What they all discovered is that the sweet wine helps pay the bills for the luxury of producing quality wines.

"We can try making Moon Puppy with it," Rosie said.

"I'm not making no frigging Moon Puppy," Gary said.

"You are a good winemaker. And I know you can do it."

The appeal to his ego was too much: You're a good winemaker. She had struck him where it hurt.

He could barely conceal his disgust when he poured his first fifty-pound bag of Domino sugar into a tub and started making sugar water.

"He added some sugar and we invited some people over and asked what do you think of this?" Rosie said. "And they said you can sell a lot of this."

But the revolt against Rosie's plans wasn't over yet. Son Tony was a commercial artist who did the wine labels for the winery. As their stepfather, Gary taught Tony and Denny how to drink wine and what constituted proper wine.

"No way am I going to do that, Mom," Rosie recalled Tony saying. So Rosie challenged him, too.

"I know you're a good commercial artist, Tony. And only you can do it."

"Tony came home one night," she recalled, "and he had this label and it was beautiful." The label showed the cartoon character of a ghostly puppy bounding happily over the moon in high, intoxicated spirits.

Then Gary had a fit when Rosie said she wanted Moon Puppy bottled in red bottles.

"They're $1.35 a bottle," he complained, while the green bottles were less than half the price at the time. And Moon Puppy was going to sell cheap compared to his quality wines.

"I want them in red bottles."

"You're crazy."

But they were bottled in red bottles.

On the day they released the wine, Gary manned the premium wine part of the counter. Rosie manned the *vin ordinaire*—meaning Moon Puppy. And when winetasters arrived, Rosie said, "All you heard was 'Moon Puppy...Moon Puppy...Moon Puppy'."

That first vintage was also judged the most perfectly balanced sweet red wine in its class that year at an annual competition of local wines in Ithaca. Perhaps that doesn't say much about the competition, but it was one more argument in favor of Moon Puppy.

So now he was adding sugar to water. It was galling in a way, but given the slim margins the winery survived on, Gary knew what he had to do if he was to keep doing what he really wanted: make dry wines.

Jason, one of Gary's temporary employees, was down on his haunches stirring the blue tub. He stirred the sugar water to the point where the sugar completely dissolved. Gary expected to add 130 pounds of sugar from the large brown bags of granulated Domino Sugar, just like the kind you use at home.

When the first batch of sugar water had fully dissolved Gary mounted his rickety widow-maker of a wooden ladder and directed Jason to dip a stainless steel bucket into the blue tub and draw up a glopping pail full of the syrup and hand it to him. Holding on to the rim of the 850-gallon stainless steel tank with one hand, Gary swung the bucket over the edge. He poured. You could hear the sugar water hit the surface of the wine with a loud cascading splash. Then there was a second bucket, and by then the tub was empty enough so that Jason picked it up in two hands and lifted it up to Gary, who grasped it while balancing precariously on the ladder with no hands and turned it on its side atop the tank rim. The remaining sugar water poured in a thick gray mass into the wine-dark sea of Moon Puppy. Bubbles floated to the surface.

Jason began mixing more sugar water. Gary placed a stainless steel clamp around a translucent hose attached to the tank. He climbed up the ladder and dropped a stainless-steel nozzle over the tank rim. Then he turned on the switch to the blue wine pump on the concrete floor. The pump sputtered and coughed as it sucked air, and then rivulets of intermittent red turned to a flood in the hoses as the pump pumped the Moon Puppy out of the bottom of the tank and back up over the top. This was Gary's low-tech answer to mixing the stew of sugar water and wine.

Later, after the wine was mixed, they went out to the tasting room. Gary brought with him two glasses of wine. One was last year's Moon Puppy. The other was the newest concoction. Jason and Shawna, who was also new at the winery and worked the counter and helped with marketing, both like sweet wines. So Gary tried the two vintages on them.

"I think this one is sweeter," Shawna said.

"No, I think the other one is," Jason said.

"It can't be."

Rosie took Shawna by the shoulders and turned her around behind the counter so she couldn't see her pour a little of each of the two Moon Puppy vintages into two new glasses.

"Now try this."

She handed the glasses to Shawna who first sniffed for the nose of a wine that normally does not deserve a bouquet, then tasted.

"I think this one is sweeter," she said. And she picked the same one.

As I had discovered, different winemakers have different philosophies. Gary has his and Chris Stamp his. Then there is Morten Hallgren. I was intrigued with Hallgren, through whom Gary had shipped the two French barrels when Hallgren was the winemaker at Dr. Frank's. I had heard that he had yet another philosophy. By the time I met him, Hallgren had opened his own winery, Ravines, located on the eastern shore of Keuka Lake.

"I'm a slow learner," he said as we sat on the balcony of his winery overlooking Keuka. One side of his mouth curled up in a mischievous grin as he mentioned his slow learning curve. Then he took a sip of French coffee. If he was slow, it's because he makes an older style of wine somewhat out of fashion

It was a brilliantly clear day in late August as the clouds flew overhead—a front had passed through the evening before, pushing the sultry air out—and now the breeze whipped up the slate-blue waves on the lake.

Morten has a vision of where wine in the Finger Lakes should go. It was very different from the others I had heard. And Moon Puppy and its kind were not a part of it.

"What's going to move the Finger Lakes forward are the drier wines," the forty-six-year-old said. And immediately he had taken on something of a holy cow among traditional grape growers in the Finger Lakes—*labrusca* grapes, the American varietals.

"How can we effectively represent Finger Lakes wines when we have such incompatible points of view within it? It's a real issue." His thick bangs had fallen across his brow, and he wore a rumpled blue cotton shirt.

He believes the Finger Lakes are ideal for making fine wine in the grand French—and not the California—tradition. In taking on California he has taken on another sacred cow.

In his view Finger Lakes wines will not be accepted in markets like New York City until they move beyond the image of sweet *labrusca*-style wines that Taylor, Gold Seal, Pleasant Valley, and Canandaigua wine companies made back in the 1950s before the California invasion of the East with *vinifera*. Back then, if you wanted *vinifera*, you bought California jug wine. If you were more upscale, you were daring and bought a French or an occasional Italian in a basket. After the last glass you could stick a candle in the rustic bottle for your Adirondack camp.

Morten makes wines that are best paired with food. It is very much a French tradition, he acknowledges, that is twenty-five to thirty years out of date considering how wine tastes have changed during the period. Yet, he believes there is a future for it and that such wines can be made in the Finger Lakes. Which, he also admits, raises the question of whether he is an anachronism or a visionary. He prefers to see himself as the latter.

"I looked very closely at the Finger Lakes and they have all the right conditions for making cool-climate *vinifera* wines," he said, which means Riesling, of course, but also Gewürztraminer, Chardonnay, as well as Cabernet Franc, and Pinot Noir for reds. Then there is Lemberger, an Austrian grape. And even Cabernet Sauvignon has a future, he believes.

One reason for Hallgren's differing perspective is because of his cosmopolitan background. He was born and raised in Denmark. In his teens, he moved to southern France, where his parents bought a winery dating back to the fourteenth century. There he learned the French wine business. "It allowed me to grow up in the business. I worked the vines. I did tours since I was sixteen years old." He headed off to college in the United States where he earned degrees in astrophysics because he wanted to figure out the universe—string theory, Big Bang, that sort of thing. He embarked on a doctorate at Boston University, then decided to cut his losses with the universe and study wine instead at a distinguished wine program in Montpelier, France. "In two weeks I went from teaching physics to taking classes in organic chemistry."

His first job as a winemaker was in Texas after he finished his wine studies. Then he did a stint as winemaker at the Biltmore Estate in Asheville, North Carolina. In 1999 he arrived in the Finger Lakes to serve as the head winemaker at the venerable Dr. Frank's. Working at

Dr. Frank's provided an awakening. "A year later I decided there was serious potential in the Finger Lakes." In 2003 he found seventeen acres at the widest point on Keuka Lake that would benefit the most from the microclimate. That's where he built his winery.

And he had a mission: To make dry *vinifera* wines but only in the lighter-bodied style like those of the French tradition in which he grew up.

"We don't aim for typical wine drinkers. We don't take the famous shotgun approach," such as that found at many wineries in the Finger Lakes where they try to appeal to the many different tastes of wine—sweet, dry, Californian. "I did not want to pursue that model."

And, he confesses, "I am out on a limb."

Still, he is not afraid to take risks. He challenges those who say there is no future for Cabernet Sauvignon or the other *vinifera* in the Finger Lakes, and he is more bullish than Gary regarding the *vinifera* varietals, even though they both are in the *vinifera* camp.

"As far as I'm concerned, there's no doubt whatsoever you can make Cabernet Sauvignon in the Finger Lakes," Morten said. It goes back to taste and the different philosophies of wine because it has to be a certain kind of wine, the kind that once dominated before California redefined reds.

"You have a whole generation that thinks that's the way wine should be. I want to make good wine that goes with good food," he said. California has a style of wine best sipped by itself. Those are the wines that win the wine-tasting contests, and they skew tasting style because they are tasted without food. What Morten cherishes is a wine derived from his experience with French winemaking. French reds were traditionally lighter bodied and more delicate, although Bordeaux hasn't hesitated to follow California in trying to cash in on the fuller-bodied American palate. Those lighter-bodied French reds don't sock you in the mouth the way a full-bodied California Cabernet Sauvignon does—robust, voluptuous, like an oversexed Marilyn Monroe newly arrived in the Golden State who is very specific about what she leaves to the imagination. True, they have their own subtle sultriness that can be nice on a cold winter's night in front of a fire in Upstate New York. But for food pairing, they aren't subtle or delicate enough—*too* voluptuous, *too* sultry, too BIG, especially during summer.

The problem, Morten says, is that California reds, which have been copied in Australia, Chile, and South Africa, lack in what's called the mid-palate. So many California reds, in his view, hit you in the mouth too quickly, overwhelming the mid-range and its own more delicate and demur palate, which the Marilyn Monroes of red wine cannot accommodate because they engage in a deliberate come-on.

So, Morten's business plan is very much at odds with the general approach in the Finger Lakes. The shotgun approach, as he calls it, means a sweet wine for those just embarking on wine drinking. And those are often made from *labrusca*. Then some hybrids are sprinkled in, which can have a faint hint of fox. And then you do *vinifera*. Morten does only *vinifera,* except for one hybrid blend, Cayuga and Vignoles. And he focuses on those cool-climate wines—demur and delicate—for what they contribute to the gustatory experience.

"California is too warm for Cabernet Sauvignon," he said, challenging convention and what for all too long has been taken for gospel. "The result is those big wines. But you can't enjoy food with them. The Finger Lakes are ideal for them."

Lest Morten's style be dismissed as an anachronism, Ravines has been described as a winery to watch by *Wine Spectator*. Nor does Morten agree, as some would have it, that *labrusca* varieties represent the beginner's gateway to good wine drinking, or that when you start drinking wine you start with something sweet the way I did as a teenager with Manischewitz Concord Grape before moving on to Boone's Farm and listening to Janis Joplin.

"I get young people here from Ithaca"—he means university students—"who appreciate dry, light-bodied wines. A lot of young people drink them. It seems to me it's an older set that tends to drink the sweet *labrusca*."

Moreover, Morten's wines have had the good fortune to land in New York City restaurants, which he sees as a vindication of his marketing plan.

He buys all Finger Lakes grapes from area vineyards. Although he recently planted five and a half acres of vines, it will be some time before they bear crop. That said, he's very picky about what he buys. Over the years he's learned which growers have grapes with distinctive and desirable characteristics. That was one advantage of working at Dr. Frank's because he bought the grapes from different growers. "What happens is you build up a mental data bank of the different qualities of grapes."

He says he is the first winemaker in the Finger Lakes to buy by the acre as opposed to weight. The result is that he can persuade vineyard owners to thin the grapes more to improve quality by concentrating more nutrients into smaller quantity. "It's more expensive that way. But the quality is much better."

He is also one of the believers in *terroir.*

"I have strong feelings about that. It's an integral part of the French school. Unfortunately it's fallen into the hands of the marketers." And, by implication, the marketers don't understand it.

By buying grapes from other growers over the years he has learned what he likes and doesn't like. "I felt I got to know different *terroir.* I cannot say I know why a *terroir* influences grapes the way they do." In Europe it has taken centuries to get to know the qualities of different *terroir.* In the Finger Lakes fine winemaking is only into its first or second generation. "We're all just starting down this road. The *terroir* of the Finger Lakes will be mapped out. But it will be generations before we understand it."

But he's already seen some evidence of its influence. For example, slate underlies much of the region. That influences Riesling, giving it a floral and white peach flavor, he said, as well as making it acidic. But he also buys Riesling from a grower on Seneca Lake who happens to grow it in a limestone area. "That has a strong minerally, citrus taste, a refreshing backbone, and is nonacidic."

"It's really about the culture you come from. I come from the French way of making wine."

It's now the end of August as George Thorogood belts out "I walked forty-seven miles of barbed wire" from the radio speaker under the roof of the crush pad at Long Point. At the same time, bottles landed with a clap and clink on the black conveyor belt; a heat compressor shrunk plastic caps over corked bottle tops; a box of bottles slid down a ramp where the "rrrip..." of packing tape sealed the box that was a moment later stacked atop cases already three high on a pallet. Clap, clink, press, slide, rrrip; clap, clink, press, slide, rrrip. There's a mechanical syncopation accompanying the music.

"By the end of this I will be dancing," Russ said with his good-natured laugh.

Dan Stevens ignored Thorogood; he had the earbud for his iPod in one ear and was listening to his own music. Chip, his yellow Labrador retriever, wandered around the edges of the crush pad with a Frisbee in his jaws, bored.

Gary was bottling Chardonnay, some 150 cases.

Peter Oughterson was placing the plastic caps over the bottles. He owns Highland Cellars and Hickory Hollow, two small wineries on the west side of Seneca Lake. More important for Gary, Peter owns the mobile wine-bottling plant, the only one in New York State, which he pulls in a box trailer hitched to an International Harvester diesel truck. By contracting out to other wineries the bottling helps to pay his bills—as well as bottle his wines. It's the equivalent of working your way through college. He's in frequent demand. In 2003 he did bottling for about twenty wineries. Now he's doing it for thirty-six. Most are in the Finger Lakes, but he also does bottling in western New York and across the border in Ontario. With short, dark brown hair and a trimmed toothbrush of a moustache, he looks like a short, muscular version of Omar Sharif.

The Chardonnay is being pumped from one of the 650-gallon stainless steel tanks inside the winery through a tangle of translucent hose.

Modern bottling is an assembly line process. It has about as much mystique as slitting a pig's guts in a slaughterhouse—methodical, mindless, eschewing the finer flights of enophile fancy. No longer are bottles filled with a funnel, then corked and labeled by hand, the way Gary used to do when he was an amateur winemaker. As an amateur Gary would call his buddies over to help, and they would liberally drink of their production while they bottled and ate garlic and hot pepper pizzas. Then it was fun. Now it's industrial. But with Peter's services, Gary can fill, cork, label, and otherwise get wine bottles ready for the wine-drinking public five times faster than he could with his own antiquated bottling machine.

Daniel Giles, a young man who wears a black tee shirt that says "Think. It's Not Illegal" and has a haystack of hair that slips out from under a baseball cap, flipped another box of empty bottles over so that they slid out right side up. There was the clap and clink on the feeder of the black conveyor belt. He arranged the bottles so they fed on to the belt, and they began their way down the conveyor into the filling chamber.

In the filling chamber they were transferred to a circle conveyor where a spout mechanically descended into each bottle mouth. Then the Chardonnay, Gary's estate, flowed in a thin stream like a translucent wine waterfall down the bottle's interior, filling up until the bottle made its circuit around the chamber.

The bottles exited the filling chamber on the conveyor belt and paused for a moment under the corking machine, which plunged a cork into each. Next the labeling machine rolled adhesive-backed labels on to the bottles. Peter placed the plastic cap over each bottle neck. The compressor throttled the cap with heat so it shrank to fit tightly for refined hands with clean fingernails to unpeel in the candlelight before removing the cork with a pop.

The bottles made their way down the length of the trailer and were inspected for imperfections in the cork, glass, and label by Dan. Any imperfections on the bottles, on average maybe 1 case out of 150, were placed in a box with a large "T" scrawled on it for tasting. They will go to the tasting room. There's nothing wrong with the wine. It's just the presentation. If the style makes the man, the same is true of wine: How it's presented anticipates the mystique of the taste.

The bottles slid down a ramp to where Russ applied the sealing tape, then picked up each case and stacked it.

From inside the winery, Gary yelled to Russ, "Tell Peter we're getting close."

"We're getting close," Russ yelled to Dan, who yelled the message back to Peter in the box trailer.

"How much?" Peter yelled back.

"How much?" Russ yelled to Gary.

"Twenty gallons."

"Pete. There's twenty gallons left," Russ yelled.

Ten minutes later, a cry went up, first one voice, then another.
"Turn it off, turn it off."
"Turn it off."
Peter turned off the pump.

Large air bubbles had appeared in the translucent pumping hose. The stainless steel tank was empty. Peter began removing the old bottle labels. Gary detached the hose from the empty stainless steel tank. He wandered about, checking hose fittings. One of the hoses had a small leak that had been fixed with the ubiquitous fixer of everything—duct tape.

Russ now picked up the Frisbee and called out, "Chip." The dog's ears pricked up as Russ took the Frisbee and sailed it across the parking lot. The dog galloped across the gravel and caught the Frisbee in his jaws, then turned around and trotted back.

Bottling may be one of the more tedious jobs at the winery. But it is also one of the most important. That's because bottles are in their own way a kind of ingredient for wine. One reason, clearly, is presentation. The other is because it gets the product to market. But there is another.

Before the seventeenth century most wine was imbibed new, meaning within the first year of vinting. That we can drink aged wines at all is due largely to the modern glass bottle, which only began to be mass-produced in the seventeenth century, and the cork, which was also introduced on a mass scale in the seventeenth century. Although the ability to blow glass bottles was known in Roman times, and glass may on occasion have been used for storing wine, it wasn't until the seventeenth century that glass manufacturing evolved to the point that bottles could be made in quantity. Before then, wine was stored in wooden barrels, which came into use in the first century AD, wine skins, or ceramic jars called *amphorae* in Greece. The biggest problem was keeping air from getting to the wine and turning it to vinegar. That's why it had to be consumed in its first year.

Not that aged wines were unknown before the seventeenth century. Enophiles have always appreciated the value of aging. As Columella wrote in about AD 60, "Almost every wine has the property of acquiring excellence with age." Some wines were aged as much as twenty-five years. But for most wine drinkers—meaning plebeians— aged wines were a rare luxury.

To preserve wine many methods were used. Wine skins were frequently covered with pitch to keep air out. And salt water or tree resin could be added to preserve the wine.

One problem with wine stored in barrels—and one that Gary remembered with his grandfather's wine—was that as the wine was drawn down, more air displaced the wine and came into contact with the remaining wine. It began to turn to vinegar. "You could barely drink it a year later." That's why the modern bottle was so important. The introduction of mass-produced bottles in the seventeenth century was not enough, however, to assure the quality of wine we generally drink today. It was the serendipitous combination with Portuguese and Spanish cork that permitted modern wine to evolve. Although cork was not unknown in classical times, for some reason it was never widely used for plugging wine containers. It may have been that because amphorae were the favored container from which to dispense wine, the openings were too large for plugging with cork. Instead, the containers were sealed with anything and everything: mud, cloth, wood, ceramic, beeswax. Even olive oil was added to top off a container. The olive oil would float on top of the wine, keeping air from getting to the vintage. Before drinking the wine, some cotton, wool or other cloth was inserted to absorb the olive oil.

But all of these methods (except perhaps for the olive oil unless the container was shaken) could not guarantee that air did not get to the wine.

Cork derives from the bark of a type of oak tree found in Portugal and Spain. It is close to ideal for sealing wine bottles, because when the bottles are stored on their sides or upside down the wine expands the cork to make a tight seal. While the absorbent cork expands, it's not entirely airproof. But it is sufficiently so, and even the small amount of air seepage can help in the aging process—what is called *microaeration.*

But cork can have its problems. According to some estimates, 2 to 5 percent of wines are ruined because of defective cork. The problem may include too much air leakage, which can occur either because the cork itself is defective or because the wine was stored upright for so long the cork dried out. Another problem, called corked wine, occurs when cork, because it is an organic material, produces a chemical compound that results in a musty wine that smells and tastes like wet newspaper or cardboard.

Such problems have prompted in recent years the development of synthetic corks. An equally important factor in that development is cost. Today, a natural cork costs about 48 cents apiece. Gary still uses cork for his better quality wines. But for his low range, such as Moon Puppy, he uses synthetic corks that cost about 11 cents each.

Some wineries are even doing what was once unthinkable and switching to screw tops, which long have been associated with cheap jug wines and fortified wines such as Thunderbird, Night Train, and Richard's Wild Irish Rose, all for the economy crowd.

Those seventeenth-century bottles posed a problem at first, too. The early ones were short, squat, and rotund, with short necks, like a Benedictine bottle, which in a sense is a direct descendent of the earlier bottles. And we still see them in the basketed Chianti bottles. Remove the basket and you have a rotund glass bottle. It's very much in shape like those early bottles. The problem with rotund wine bottles during this early period was that they were hard to store on their sides to ensure that the cork absorbed the wine and expanded to form a seal. This was remedied by changing the shape of the bottle. It was elongated so that it could lie on its side. By 1760, the modern wine bottle had taken shape: It was long and skinny.

The result of combining mass-produced glass bottles with cork is that winemaking has never been the same. Indeed, it's difficult to know how wines tasted before the seventeenth century because of such improvements as the bottle and cork.

Beaming over the airwaves from land of the dead, the voice of Bob Marley reggaed, "I shot the sheriff..."

Dan brought out the hand forklift, inserted the forks under the pallet of boxed Chardonnay, raised it, and backed it into the winery. Gary attached the hose to the Cabernet Franc tank.

Peter was taking partially filled bottles from the filling chamber and pouring them into a stainless steel bucket. Gary attached a new hose that ran from the filter back to the Cabernet Franc tank. The Chardonnay had to be flushed out of the hose. Gary will recycle it back into the Cabernet Franc since the law allows up to 25 percent of other wines to be mixed in and you can still label it by the name of the dominant varietal.

Levi rinsed out the buckets.

Bob Marley continued, "And they say it is a capital offence…"

Russ picked up the Frisbee and threw it out into the parking lot. This time Chip didn't bring it back. He took it to Dan instead. Dan leaned over and hugged the dog. Then Dan walked out into the parking lot and threw the Frisbee. The dog gave chase.

Peter prepared to add more corks and new labels. "How many gallons of Cab Franc?" he called out.

Russ, at the entrance to the winery, called into Gary, who stood on an aluminum extension ladder removing the temporary hose he had recycled the Chardonnay with: "How many gallons should we have?"

"450," Gary responded from the top of the tank.

"450 gallons," Russ confirmed and walked away to tell Peter.

After the Chardonnay had been recycled Gary reconnected the hoses to the bottling line. Then the production line dance began again: clap, clink, press, slide, rrrip….

But now it was to the Latin moves of Santana, "Ain't got nobody that I can depend on…"

"My iPod just shuffled from Dave Matthews to Johnny Cash," Dan Stevens volunteered. No one responded as they went through their mechanical motions.

Santana continued, "Ain't got no one tengo a nadie…"

There's a sense in early September that everything is imminent. It's still summer, but a summer on the wane, and in a few weeks harvesting will begin.

In the vineyard Joe looked like an extraterrestrial on the Case tractor driving through the vine rows. This was in the early years. He wore a white Tyvek suit with a white hood over his head. A respirator, the kind with two canisters jutting out diagonally from the nose, covered his face. The canisters suggested two pincers ready to grab terrestrial prey.

Joe leaned to one side and looked over his shoulder as he drove the tractor up between the rows. Behind him rose the loud whine of the fogger as it sprayed a low, earth-hugging cloud of fungicide at the base of the grapevines. Joe the Martian alternated between looking over his shoulder and steering the tractor. The sprayer was on loan from King Ferry.

He arrived at the end of the row, throttled the tractor, and made a wide sweeping turn so that the tractor disappeared into an alley two rows up—he didn't have the turning radius to go to the next alley over between rows. That's the way he sprayed, weaving through one alley, then moving up two alleys. Then he'll drop back down to the rows he's skipped.

The grapes had matured. You saw it in the Cabernet Franc. You saw it when you turned the corner to come down the side road to the winery entrance and all of a sudden, hanging from the bottom of the vines, were dark, almost black clusters of Cabernet Franc, bunches of them hanging from the vines. They looked succulent, and it's easy to imagine lying under the vines and reaching up to pluck a grape with your teeth in a Dionysian reverie, your back baking on the warm earth.

The grapes had reached *veraison,* the point when they cease being hard like peas. Now they took on their harvest color and began juicing up. One could suck the juice out of them now, but it would be tart and sour—and covered with fungicide. Perhaps most important, the grapes were beginning to build up their sugar content: The more sugar, the more alcohol, and the more alcohol, the more stable the wine so it won't turn to vinegar.

The Chardonnay too had reached *veraison.* While the Cab Franc come close in size to conventional red table grapes, the Chardonnay are much smaller, more like small marbles.

Yet, trying to get a sense of the harvest can still be elusive, especially in a confounding year. This year, as Joe sprayed, the grapes were still at least two weeks behind. But they promised to be particularly juicy because of rain. So in spite of the hardships of a growing season it could still turn out to be a good year. It depends on the sun and the manufacture of sugar in the grapes.

"If we have an early frost, we could lose most of it. If the weather stays warm, it could be a great harvest," Gary said.

A couple of weeks later, Joe was down in the Chardonnay block again driving the Case tractor while looking over his shoulder. Behind him, on a staging platform bolted to the tractor, Cyrus, a dark, lean eighteen-year-old, held on to the knotted end of black nylon fishnet mesh that unrolled now from the opposite end of the first row of vines. They were covering the rows of grapevines to protect clusters from birds and deer. This was before coverage of the vines during the growing season became a routine practice.

"John's down in the rows with his crew covering the grapes," Joe called out above the din of the tractor engine. "We've done about half the rows."

He was referring to John Balliett, the vineyardist at King Ferry Winery. Even though both King Ferry and Long Point had erected electrified fences, they don't always stop the deer. Deer can do considerable damage to a grape crop. Now John was helping Joe. It's the exchange of labor bred by the familiarity small family wineries have with each other—*have* to have with each other. One has this piece of equipment, the other has that. And both need each other's manpower because of a perennial shortage of skilled hands.

There was a sense of urgency to covering the grapes. A gray sultriness sat over the Finger Lakes region. While there was a patch of blue overhead, clouds had locked it in a kind of atmospheric vise. There was a stiff, warm breeze blowing from the west. And on the far side of Cayuga Lake maybe four miles away the middle air between earth and cloud had dissolved in an opaque wall of rain moving slowly this way. Already, one could hear the distant guttural grumble of thunder. There was going to be a sudden unburdening of the sky.

Joe had reached the end of the vine row. Such was how he measured out the length of netting for each row of vines. Now he put the tractor in reverse as Cyrus fed the nylon fishnet into a large blue fifty-gallon plastic barrel attached to the back of the tractor. Slowly, Joe backed to the beginning of the row where he had started unrolling the fourteen-foot-wide roll of mesh.

Like so much at the winery, there is a lot of improvisation. The nylon feeder is home-built. Joe had shoved a street-sign pole through the cardboard roller holding the net, and placed the pole ends atop pallets stacked three high.

Once he had measured the mesh, he drove the tractor down to the next row of grapes in the vineyard to be covered.

With a graying head of wild hair tousled by a storm wind and a graying handlebar moustache that suggested a merry French raconteur, John Balliet happily made his political prejudices known: "Wine is made on the vine." Again, the old argument between vineyardist and winemaker, and John was staking out his territory.

But doesn't that depend on the grape? I asked. Some are ripe for wine on the vine, some need the help of the winemaker.

John won't yield his ground. "No, it depends on how well the vineyardist takes care of his vines."

To hear John tell it, then, vineyardists are the unsung heroes of winemaking.

John placed the ball of the knotted end of nylon mesh over the anchoring post to the row of vines and stooped down to tie it under, over, and around the fruiting wires. Joe eased the hand clutch into gear and the tractor took off at a brisk walking pace as Henry, a fourteen-year-old on his first summer job, pulled the mesh through a piece of six-inch PVC plumbing pipe. As the netting fed out John took it in hand and draped it loosely over the vines. On the other side of the row, "B-Man"—John's eleven-year-old son, Brendan—grasped the mesh hand over hand so that it draped evenly over on his side.

At the end of the row the knotted end of the mesh passed through the PVC pipe. The tractor paused, then Joe throttled and returned with Cyrus back up to the roll of mesh to unroll another vine-row length.

The chatter of the tractor gone, John, Henry, and B-Man were reminded of the coming storm by another rumble. John and the boys headed back down to the beginning of the row and started tugging the net down and along the length of the vines to take up the slack. They moved quickly. The thunder sounded, echoing from out of Finger Lakes country to the west. Suddenly, B-man cried out, "The net's ripped. The net's ripped." At eleven, he was all work and little child's play, even though he wears a black baseball cap backwards on his head reminding me of a rapper of the vineyards.

"The net's ripped," John yelled out, as much to the coming storm as to anyone in particular. "Quick. Find the ends. Damn."

With B-Man and Henry they searched for the ends that had bunched up in careless folds so it was hard to tell what was what. Unraveling the net, they pulled the two ends together and clipped them with spring-loaded clothespins.

Then the boys began working their way down the length of the green canopy, one on each side, clothespinning the two sides of the fishnet mesh at the bottom of the row near ground level.

"We need one here," John said as he checked their work.

Thunder sounded in the distance, and the mass of opaque gray that joined land and cloud had now turned to char over the lake, an impenetrable wall of char connecting water and sky. It looked like the lake was being sucked up into the Heavens at the command of some Old Testament prophet.

"It's coming this way," John said, perceiving divine intent.

When they finished pinning the row the vines looked like they were encased in black fishnet stocking, which in a sense they were.

John is another escapee from nine-to-five. He once managed the estates of the inventor of the credit card—"He makes two cents on every transaction," John said enviously. He gave it up to become a vineyardist in his brother-in-law's winery some eight years before.

"I love it. I love working outdoors. I wouldn't do anything else."

But it sounded like a script for a newspaper reporter; something else remained undefined, I sensed. John had been an estate manager. Joe had been an aircraft technician. One of Gary's employees was a computer programmer. Gary is a nuclear medicine technician. Rosie, well, Rosie is the long-suffering one. She's doing it for Gary. Or so she says. Then there are the doctors and lawyers who have been willing, so they told Gary, to work for low wages, reading a memorized script on the virtues of Gary's wines while giving wine tastings—like demigods providing entrance into the mysteries of the vine. It made me think of some outpost of the French Foreign Legion. Each has his own past that he has left behind—or would like to leave behind—having escaped the illusions he once chose to believe in. It's as if amid the vines, one can find peace of mind in the production of the perfect vintage that is as much an illusion as any. Except that, unlike the routines of nine-to-five, the mysteries of wine multiply.

Joe reappeared with another length of net to install, and the tractor moved up to the next row and Joe fed the net and John drove the tractor. Then, in the distance over the lake, a long seam of needle-thin, sharp-edged lightning sliced swiftly through the sky, a reminder of the connection between Heaven and Earth, and now the thunder could be heard above the tractor's chatter.

"We have ten minutes," John yelled from the seat of the tractor. Another thin seam of lightning agreed, striking over the lake.

The storm breeze swelled with the sweet scent of late summer hay, and for a moment the netting billowed above the row of vines. It was if they were tucking a baby in to sleep as they joined opposite edges of mesh together underneath the vines with clothespins. Then everyone converged on joining the mesh together, Joe, John, Henry, Cyrus.

"Henry, go get the snacks," John said as soon as the net was joined. "B-man, get on the tractor." John mounted the seat, and the tractor took off up the hill where a gate had to be closed. John's son held on to the mesh-feeding pole as the tractor lurched from one side to the other. Another sudden slender needle of lightning ripped through the gray rain between the cloud above and the lake below.

At the gate, John hopped down and ran to close it. He locked the gate and bounded up to the tractor. He headed down the vine row to the other open gate. There he and his son joined Joe, Henry, and Cyrus.

"I'm out of here," B-Man said, and on his first job at the age of eleven he seemed to relish no longer playing a kid. The thunder cackled loudly now, not more than a mile away. They headed out of the vineyard at a fast walk, Joe staying behind to secure the gate.

A few minutes later everyone had gathered outside the winery. The storm was coming in with light sprays of rain, and the crew laughed with a sense of relief and talked among themselves. In a few minutes the full force of the rain would arrive.

And most of the grapes, having reached *veraison,* were now safely tucked in.

King Ferry Winery, and its owners, Pete and Tacie Saltonstall, had always loomed large in the life of Long Point Winery. Pete loaned Gary his equipment, as well as his hired help, and even his storage space during the winter for Gary's old Case tractor. In the world of commercial competition such generosity may appear naïve, no matter how passionate the enophilia. Yet there it was.

As a mature winery, King Ferry provided a striking comparison to Long Point. It's the kind of winery Gary hoped his would be some day. A few days after the storm, John took me on a tour of the vines in a golf cart. There was no humidity and the air felt crisp but warm under the direct sunlight. There were more days like this. Puffy clouds moved sluggishly across the sky, still a reminder of summer, which yet had a week to go.

The King Ferry vineyards were divided by a wooded stream with neatly arranged green rows of vines wandering off to either side, disappearing over rises, dipping, then continuing to borders of trees down at the bottom of the slope. Beyond sat the tranquil waters of Cayuga Lake. There were vines and grapes wherever you looked. Here, among the rows, there was an intimacy, a solace from the "madding crowd." The Gewürztraminer and Riesling clusters hung heavily with fruit. Yet John was apologetic about his twenty-two-plus acres of vineyard.

"I would like mine to look like Joe's," he said. "I haven't been able to keep down the weeds."

He pointed at the bottom of the vines where there were weedy infestations, strange, yellow-looking creatures with thistles and burrs and other distressing dress whose roots rob the grapes of nutrients.

"Ideally, I would like all that out down to the ground."

The problem comes back to the lack of labor in the region.

"You need one man for every ten acres," John said.

Right now it's just him and a teenager working part-time.

Nor can John spray with a pesticide—a quick fix for weeds. It's too close to harvest and the window for spraying had closed. The grapes would absorb the pesticide in twenty-four hours and might not break down chemically in time for picking.

In an alley between the Gewürztraminer, John stopped the golf cart. The grapes were covered with nylon netting. His vineyards are surrounded by an electric fence to keep out deer. Still, he covers the grapes. A few days before he discovered about twenty-five wild turkeys had flown into the vineyard. Despite the explosion from a gas cannon punctuating the air every few minutes and designed to frighten them, they were feasting on his grapes. He put up the mesh to protect the remainder.

Even the electric fence doesn't stop the deer because the scent of the sugar drives them crazy. "They will keep trying to jump it, and when they hit the fence they're stunned for a moment and then will come back and try it again." The previous week a deer finally succeeded in crashing through the fence, despite the electrification, because it was so crazed by the smell of ripening grapes.

John lifted the netting and plucked a grape. He squeezed the bottom of it so that the juice and pulp popped out at the stem end and on to his tongue. "You can taste the sweetness, but it's still not there."

He offered one. Indeed, it was sweet but with an acidic and sour aftertaste.

"We were pretty naïve when we got into this," Pete Saltonstall told me a little later at the winery. Pete is a big man whose stature belies his almost deferential tone punctuated with a frequent carefree laugh. The laugh reminds you of a big, happy Labrador retriever who likes to lope playfully about, perhaps chasing the elusive Frisbee except that Pete's bad back won't let him.

Part of the reason Pete is so supportive of Gary is the fraternity they form, the shared enthusiasm they have for their subject, Pete said. They like to talk wine. But there is another reason. "This is a little bit selfish," Pete said. "I'd love to have more wineries on this side of the lake. I'd like to see four. Over at Fox Run," which is on the west side of Seneca, "they tell me they have anywhere from 100,000 to 110,000 visitors a year. Here, our best guess is 20,000 to 25,000 a year."

The more wineries there are, presumably the more tasting traffic there will be. Some 60,000 customers, according to New York State, visit the fourteen wineries just on the west side of Cayuga Lake annually. But again, on the east side of Cayuga until recently there were only two wineries at mid-lake, Long Point and King Ferry, while at the north end there was Montezuma, and at the south end, Six Mile Creek. Since I met Peter three more wineries have opened, all north of Long Point on Route 90.

There is also an object lesson in what has happened over on Seneca Lake, Pete suggested. "There's some talk that it's become overdeveloped." After all, how many flights can a wine taster drink in an afternoon of driving and tasting?

King Ferry opened for business in 1989. Given what's happened in recent years the Saltonstalls got in on the craft winery phenomenon early. But Pete and Tacie were different from Gary and Rosie. They were young and just starting a family—Pete was only thirty when he and Tacie made the decision in the early 1980s to start the winery. He had been successful in the construction business and had an inheritance. Down in the King Ferry vineyard in knee-high weeds sits a vestige of Pete's former life—an abandoned panel truck now used for storage and announcing in a flourishing but fading script across the side, "Saltonstall Construction."

He left that career behind and chose wine for his next, becoming one more refugee from the monotony of the existential assembly line, one who now gets to frolic to his heart's content in the vineyard of the soul.

Except it hasn't been easy.

"I remember Tacie being seven, eight months pregnant riding a cultivator and wondering, what was she doing out there?" Pete said. "She was pregnant. She should have been home being pregnant. Not working in a vineyard."

 AUTUMN

HARVEST SKIES IN UPSTATE are skies of passage. Autumn in the Finger Lakes—like spring—is not long. Rather, there's a sudden decompression of the universe, as summer rushes pell-mell, against its best interests, into the cold embrace of winter. You can't even call autumn an interlude, with all the poignancy and respite that an interlude suggests. It's too grim for that, as people "go down the cellar" to get the storms, change the oil in the snow thrower, and brace themselves for the months of gray skies and snow. Simply, there's too much to do and no time to reflect on the passage.

That's how it is at the winery and in the vineyard, too. Reflection will have to wait until winter.

Dan walked down the alley between two Riesling rows. He stopped, unclipped the netting, lifted and folded it over the grapevines, and selected from the middle of a tight cluster one white grape, with little red cheeks bussed by the chilly nights. He plucked the grape from the stem, opened a plastic sandwich bag, and dropped it in. Now he had five grapes. He placed the bag in the kangaroo pouch of his sweatshirt, lowered the netting, and reattached it at the bottom. He continued down the row. He had thirty-one more rows to go.

It was a cool, but not uncomfortable, autumn day, and the sun moved in and out from lines of silver clouds drifting east. When Dan reached near the end of the row, he unclipped the netting, and picked another grape. But this time he selected from the end of the cluster. "What I try to do is pick berries from different locations in the cluster. That way I get a broader sample."

September had given way to October, and he was preparing to test for sugar content and pH in the Riesling, which would help determine if the grapes were ready to pick. Gary would also determine if they had the right taste—he has the final say. It depends on the personal preferences of the vintner's taste buds.

Dan began sampling two weeks earlier to establish a baseline and now he was nervous because he wanted to get the grapes picked. But the sugar content had to be right.

During the first sampling at the end of September there was still a touch of summer to the air. The Riesling that time came in at nineteen Brix; Gary considers twenty-three optimum. So there was still room for improvement. But that first testing was followed by a week and a half of cold rain and frosts. And the vines were taking the hint.

"The plants are beginning to shut down," Gary told me.

Dan originally anticipated picking toward the end of October. Now, as he collected his second sample, he faced the prospect of picking the Riesling sooner. He walked up and down each alley, picking three grapes at random from each of the thirty-three rows of Riesling to get his hundred-berry sample. Then there were the Chardonnay and Pinot Gris to do. In some ways it's a slow, leisurely process, surrounded by vines heavy with grape clusters. "This is like the employee exercise program. It's a lot of walking," Dan said.

You could see the evidence of the plants shutting down in the vine leaves: They had started to tinge with yellow. In another telltale sign, little black rings started to appear in the skin around the berry stems. The grapes were no longer receiving nutrients from the vine. There was also some botrytis—not enough to destroy the crop, but it had to be watched in case it became aggressive. And if it did, there was nothing that could be done.

"Gary, I can't spray at this point," Dan said the week before, as the winemaker's anxiety increased each day amid the cold and rain.

"It's not under control but it's not rampant," Dan told me. "It's about one or two clusters per vine. But if it gets out of control, there's nothing I can do to stop it."

This is also the time of year when neighboring farms are bringing in or have already brought in their crops. Pumpkins, gourds, cabbage, corn, soybeans—the bounty of Upstate, which is a rich agricultural belt, was coming out of the fields and going to market. You can see it in the big farm trucks hurtling down Route 90 loaded with crop. Chaff from trucks loaded with newly harvested soybeans whirls out, covering the windshields of cars behind with soy sap. It's a reminder of just how close to the edge *vinifera* grape growers live. As Joe once said, "Around here, farmers put their crops in after we begin pruning the grapes, and harvest their crops before we harvest ours."

Now Dan was into October collecting his sample as he walked his "employee exercise program." He thinks the grapes should be picked immediately.

"Things are really, really close, and they're at that point where I think they are a lot higher than what other people have decided to start bringing in," Dan said, referring to the level of sugar in the grapes.

The "other people" are the other vineyardists and winemakers in the Finger Lakes.

"It's all because of these, I don't know, maybe unrealistic expectations."

He was trying to be polite because it's not nice to criticize your boss by name. Did he mean winery owners?

"Yeah," he said, and he laughed. "If he," meaning Gary, "were actually growing, he would have more of a—I guess I feel like he should have more of an understanding of being in my position and watching things start to degrade."

He neared the end of the row, unclipped the net, folded it up, and took a grape from behind the cluster close to the stem. He dropped it in his plastic bag.

When to pick is an ancient argument. The vineyardist and the winemaker watch closely the weather forecasts this time of year. Choosing the best time to pick is no easier than deciphering Sanskrit. At the moment the forecast is discouraging, calling for rain and mostly cloudy conditions the rest of the week, with nighttime temperatures continuing to dip into the mid-thirties. Now the vineyardist and vintner are in a race with the weather, as they nervously watch the autumn skies, gambling that they can get the crop in before it's too late.

Of course, if the grapes are not sweet enough—if the Brix content is not high enough—the vintner can always add sugar. But in a perfect world it's something they do not want to do given that wine is supposed to be an entirely natural product. Does it make a difference in taste? Gary says he can tell the difference. Still, it happens that a crop comes in and the sugar content is too low and a winemaker wants to save his crop. And it's a reminder of the shifting boundaries of enological correctness.

Dan continued up an alley, taking his samples. The air was broken by the sound of starlings. Then grackles. For the bird life it sounded as if it were August or the beginning of September. The strange part was that you didn't see them. As Dan moved toward the center of the Riesling block, the sounds of the birds increased in volume. Then you saw the loudspeaker raised just above the level of the vine tops. It was new, and the sound convincing. Grackles and starlings are aggressive, and the recording was designed to frighten off other birds.

In the middle of the Riesling vineyard Dan came on a vine with, inexplicably, red grape clusters.

"I don't know what it is," he said. "But it's not uncommon to find another variety. When you get the plantings, it happens that other plantings get mixed in by mistake."

When he worked at Sheldrake Point Vineyard across the lake he recalled how one year the Riesling was decimated by eight days of rain. After the rain he went out to remove grape clusters heavily damaged by botrytis and sour rot.

"You were walking down a row, and all of sudden you could see this big, beautiful, totally clean cluster, and you asked, what the heck is happening?"

While the rain had murdered the Riesling, one vine flourished, with plump white clusters. They sent off a sample to Geneva and it came back identified as Vidal Blanc, the French hybrid.

"And Vidal Blanc looks a lot like Riesling," Dan said.

Whatever the identity of the red grape we walked by, it would be left to hang and get picked when the Cabernet Franc are picked and blended with those. The amount was too small to make a difference in taste or the labeling of the wine. All of which makes you wonder about what constitutes truth in wine, not so much in terms of the ancient adage but in terms of contents.

"I don't believe in truth in wine," Dan scoffed. "For example, when you make beer you want perfect conditions. You sterilize everything. It's got to be perfect. But in wine, it's no big deal, when you think about it. I mean, look, there's bird shit on these grapes, let's be honest. There'll be spiders, there'll be bugs, there'll be fruit flies."

And so it has been, ever since Noah was credited with making the first wine (and getting soused). Does that mean wine is not clean? No. It's filtered, and the fermentation process and resulting alcohol kill off the microscopic bad guys. This is why in classical times wine was the beverage of choice, at least in Greece and Rome. After all, sources of drinking water often could not be trusted. At the time of Jesus, it's estimated that Rome, a city of more than a million people, consumed 1.8 million hectoliters (180 million liters) of wine a year. That averages out to half a liter a day for every inhabitant of the city, including infants. Aside from serving the occasional bacchanalian revel (the government eventually banned the rites of Bacchus in Rome because they got too wild), wine served the more important purpose of being potable. Certainly the Tiber River wasn't.

Farther down the row now, Dan unclipped the net, lifted it, and took another berry sample.

"These actually taste really, really good. Try one of these," he said.

They were at the southern end of the vine row where they were exposed to more sunlight. "It's got some really good tropical fruit flavors," he said.

We tasted. He observed that at the northern end of the row the fruit was more acidic because it was less mature. But the combination of the different results at the two ends of the row should mean a good Riesling, he said. These variables—the differences of soil, sun, and air currents that are part of the *terroir* on the east shore of Cayuga Lake—contribute to the vintage.

Later, at the lab in the winery, Dan crushed the grapes in the bag, kneading them with his hands until what was left was a soggy pulp. He poured the juice from the bag into a tall beaker. He inserted a long hydrometer as Gary walked in and asked, "How does it look?"

The hydrometer read eighteen Brix. It had gone down a Brix from when Dan did the first sampling two weeks earlier, undoubtedly because of the rain. Not encouraging.

Then Dan used a refractometer. Dan and Gary have an ongoing disagreement as to which is more accurate, the hydrometer or the refractometer. Dan said that the hydrometer, which winemakers frequently use, is notoriously inaccurate because the solids in the juice throw off the reading. But in the past, Gary found that once grapes were crushed, and the solids separated, the Brix content was always higher than what a refractometer revealed, and so the hydrometer was more accurate.

Now Dan squeezed an eyedropper in the juice, extracted a drop, and deposited a smear of juice on the prism of the refractometer, which is the size of a small flashlight. He closed the glass slide over the prism and held the refractometer up to one eye with two hands the way a pirate might hold a spyglass.

"Seventeen Brix."

What you saw through the prism resembled the way the earth shades part of the moon in a half-moon, a shadowy line, the difference between night and day, crossing the 17 on the scale in the prism. To Gary it proved his point: The hydrometer gave a higher reading. To Dan it proved his: The hydrometer was inaccurate.

"I don't care—if it gets the grapes picked sooner," Dan said later.

What they did agree on is that the vines were shutting down. The season was coming to an end. And even if Gary did not approve of the taste of the grapes—likely still too acidic although Riesling benefits from acid—they had to be picked. But Dan was unhappy because Gary could get pickers to pick on the coming Friday or Saturday, and Gary won't do it.

"It's one of the busiest weekends of the year," Gary said, because it was Columbus Day weekend. "There's too much going on." Namely in terms of sales and the imperative that you have to sell what you make.

Dan saw it differently: "If the fruit has to come off, it has to come off. Who cares if it's busy in the tasting room. You can't schedule the weather. You can't control certain things. If you can't control it, you shouldn't try."

Of course Gary could turn the argument around: If you can't control it, what difference does a few days make? Also, to Gary there was something else: "You can add sugar, but you can't add ripe flavors." And he wants the flavors as ripe as possible. So, Gary wouldn't budge: the Riesling (and Pinot Gris) would be picked the following Columbus Day Monday—a full week after testing for sugar.

During harvest, I noticed, there always seemed to be a turbulence to the skies. When the first crop of Riesling was harvested at Long Point, the sun ducked in and out from behind clouds that came in gray, silver-lined waves like frothy ocean swells from out of the west. Leading them were high cumulus that appeared as billowing sails of ships running before the wind, trying to outrun the storm.

I recall one harvest day several years ago when early in the morning the sun rose in a crystalline sky, except for a long, even line of clouds far off to the west. By nine o'clock the long line had become a sodden-looking quilt of dark gray moving across the sky, bringing with it a sense of impending foul weather that everyone hoped would hold off until the evening as they went about harvesting the grapes. Soon, blue skies were more a memory far off to the east.

Gary has only one realistic option for picking grapes, which is to hire Mexican farm laborers, an informal group of up to half a dozen or so—the precise number depending on who is available at the moment. But that's if Gary can get them. They are in constant demand because they are the most skilled group of pickers in the area. If he can't get them he has to depend on the message getting out by word-of-mouth to friends, relatives, locals. He will call Pete at King Ferry to borrow (and pay) some of his workers. The going rate is $2.50 a lug, up from $2 a lug when his Chardonnay, his first harvest, was picked in 2002. And there are the times when he and Dan have been down in the vineyard picking because there were too few pickers.

It can lead to some tense moments when he can't get enough skilled workers. The year the sodden gray clouds eclipsed the sun, it seemed at first that he might have only one picker, a local, who appeared at the brow of the hill around nine in the morning, buffeted by the autumn gusts as he walked down to the vineyard, leaning into the cold wind. Gary could only pray that more followed. They did, in a couple of hours, showing up in ones and twos, and the crop got picked.

The season the Riesling were first harvested the grapes went from "gangbusters" to simply "good," as Dan put it (but he characterized the Cabernet Franc as "wicked good"). He didn't want to get his hopes up because of the early cold rains. As it turned out, holding off picking saw the Riesling rise to 20.5 Brix by the time they were picked and crushed. Not 23, Gary's standard, but better than 17 or 18.

For Dan, that meant more meatballs.

"I told him, for each additional Brix, he gets one of Rosie's home-made meatballs," Gary said.

Dan laughed. "Oh, and Rosie makes the best Italian meatballs."

I had caught up with them at the crush pad. They were crushing the last of the Pinot Gris—which, in the end, would come in at 22.5 Brix. Dan, Russ, and Levi unloaded yellow plastic lugs and dumped their contents into the crusher, which crushed and destemmed the grapes.

A cascade of Pinot Gris descended into the trough of the crusher, where a long screw pushed them into the maw. From there the juice, pulp, and skins—the grape "must"—were pumped to the press while the stems were carried away by a reverse screw to be ejected from the back of the crusher into a plastic tub.

Gary and Dan also had a bet on tonnage. Dan said the Riesling would top out at more than ten tons.

"Nah, it's going to be eight or nine," Gary said. At stake were more meatballs. Gary would win this bet. But Rosie was generous and made a plate of meatballs for Dan anyway.

They finished dumping the lugs. Dan climbed into the cab of the Bobcat tractor Gary had bought recently to replace the old Case when the steering gave out. Levi mounted the trailer, steadying himself against the stacked yellow lugs. They were taking them back down to the vineyard where the Mexican workers were starting to pick the Riesling.

José Aguilera reached with his open clippers into the leaves, placed the forked blades around the stem, and squeezed the handles. The Riesling cluster dropped into the near empty yellow lug on the ground beneath. He worked quickly, mechanically, stooping slightly and leaning into the vines. He inserted his clippers into the leaves again, lodged the forked blades around another stem, and squeezed. Again the cluster dropped softly to the lug, which slowly filled up with the fruit of the vine.

So it went, the eyes intimate with veined leaves, the coarse, abrasive bark of the vines, and the burnished faces of grapes, the hand reaching into the vines, pushing the leaves aside, the clippers wrapping around the stems. The quick "clip" and the sound of grapes dropping through the rustle of leaves, landing in the lug.

José was twenty-four, tall and slender, with a long, refined nose and a dark, neatly trimmed Vandyke beard. Like most of the pickers, he is from the state of Michoacán in south central Mexico adjacent to the Pacific Coast. He comes from a farming district and arrived in the United States when he was eighteen to work as an agricultural laborer. Ever since, José has worked in agriculture, and he is one of the informal leaders of the group of Mexican pickers. Fluent in English, José is fortunate in some ways because he met a young American woman and now they are married, giving him easier entrée into American society.

While they pick, the Mexican pickers may think of their families in Mexico or the exigencies of daily life that everyone deals with, such as the milk to pick up after work. "But usually there's no time to think," José said, because thinking slows them down, which translates into lost wages. Nor is there much conversation among them in the vineyard, in part for the same reason, but also because they fan out to stake their own territory.

Local pickers approach picking differently. Unlike the Mexican pickers, the initial silence for the Americans can give way to a casual if temporary camaraderie that accompanies the clip-drop, clip-drop repetitiveness that has the effect of lowering the barriers between those who have never met before. On one harvest, John Chandler, who was helping pick, and Jessica Pickert, a ceramicist from Bainbridge, worked on opposite sides of a row and for some reason started talking about hot chili peppers.

"I think my favorite is chipotles. They have flavor you can taste," John said as he snipped a stem and the grape cluster dropped. As with many who lead other lives but long for life amid the vines, he was a research scientist in biochemistry at Cornell who helped out occasionally at Long Point because some day he, too, hoped to start his own winery. For him it was a learning experience. Now, on a day of penetrating cold, he was more intent on chili peppers. "The only kind I don't like are jalapeños."

"Yeah. They don't have much flavor," Jessica said, her hand amid the vine leaves, holding in her palm a grape bunch. She snipped and withdrew the bunch, placing it in the lug. "I like chipotles, too. But have you ever had——," and she named a chili pepper so strange to the ear it sounded impossible to spell, like the name of some exotic Mayan goddess with lots of x's. They continued to talk of chili peppers the way some people talk of wine.

Dan had now returned to the Riesling block with lugs for José and his crew. Dan, Russ, and Levi unloaded the lugs, each dispersing them to a different row, dropping one every twenty feet or so to await the pickers.

José found a cluster too far recessed in the leaves. With his right hand he pushed the leaves aside and took the cluster in the other hand. He tugged, raising the cluster to reveal the stem. Rapidly, the clippers severed the stem. José withdrew the cluster from the vines in the palm of his hand and dropped it in the lug.

By the time the pickers had started on the Riesling, they could feel the temperature slowly dropping and the wind picking up.

"The worst is when it rains and it gets cold," José said. That happened during a harvest when the Riesling were picked at King Ferry. It was a steady rain. The temperature was in the fifties, which at first didn't seem cold. And the rain brought out the sweet smell of hay in the neighboring field. But because it didn't take long to get soaked, even if you wore waterproof raingear, the cold began to penetrate. Most of the Mexican pickers worked without raingear. One was dressed only in a saturated short-sleeved polo shirt, almost a wet rag, clinging to his arms and chest. He loaded lugs on a farm wagon, indifferent to the rain. In the distance the outline of Cayuga Lake was battleship gray. It disappeared into a miasma of rain and clouds, a study in gray fading into gray fading into gray.

The Bobcat arrived at the crush pad towing the first load of Riesling. It pulled up in front of the crusher.

Dan and Gary stacked six lugs on a scale. They topped out at 171 pounds, or 28.5 pounds per box. With 56 lugs, that was about 1,600 pounds. Gary wrote it down on a clipboard.

Gary pushed the switch for the crusher and the chain drive rattled while the screw impeller began to turn, pleading for grapes. Dan picked up a lug from the trailer. Russ did too, then Levi. Dan carried his over to the crusher and raised it above the long, coffin-like bin in which the impeller turned. He tilted it and large masses of grapes— almost white in color but with flashes of light green and rust— descended into the impeller, which carried them into the stainless steel crusher. Soon a light green slurry of grape must poured from a hose into the top of the wine press. Gary dug into a hundred-pound paper bag of rice hulls and pulled from it a filled plastic cup. He poured the hulls into the press. The rice hulls filter out solids when the grape must is pressed.

Russ heaved a lug over the crusher edge so vigorously that some clusters dropped from the opposite side.

"You went a little over on that one," Dan said.

I tasted a Riesling grape, squeezing the bottom so the juice came out from stem end, followed by the pulp. It was deliciously sweet, as much or more so than table grapes. Dan said they had a lot of acid. I couldn't taste it. The skins were tough, chewy, a little leathery, unlike table grapes.

The lugs empty, Dan left on the tractor to take them back to the pickers and load another round. This time, too, Gary had placed a large cardboard bin with a plastic liner on the trailer. It's designed to carry a ton of grapes. He was looking for ways to speed up the processing and was worried the pickers could run out of lugs. The lugs would be emptied into the box down in the vineyard and left for the pickers to reuse.

Gary poured a last cup of rice hulls into the press, then sealed the doors. The press is a huge stainless steel cylinder designed to hold up to two and a half tons of fresh grapes. Gary stepped back and flipped the switch on the air compressor. He reached forward and turned the valve on the wine press. You could hear the press groan and stretch as the air filled the white synthetic balloon-like diaphragm inside. When the pressure reached twenty-five pounds per square inch, the press shut off.

Inside, the diaphragm expanded, forcing the juice through the filter of rice hulls, which had been pushed outward by the pressure. The juice began to trickle into the press basin and out a drain from which it was pumped into the tallest of the stainless steel tanks.

Gary watched the pressure gauge. Twenty-five pounds per square inch is the maximum recommended pressure for that press. As the diaphragm displaced the juice the pressure slowly declined. When it reached twenty pounds per square inch, the cylinder rotated and the air pump kicked in and the pressure climbed. It stopped at twenty-five. The juice continued to trickle into the basin.

The Mexican workers finished picking the Riesling by mid-afternoon. They were paid by check and left for the next job. "And they all have green cards," Gary seemed to make a point of emphasizing. The last thing he wanted was Immigration showing up.

The crushing and pressing continued until after midnight.

In Italy, there is an old mosaic ceiling in a former Roman temple from the fourth century AD that celebrates the harvest. In one corner a farmhand prepares to pour a basket of grapes into a farm cart. In another, in a stone basin covered by a tent-like structure, two men crush grapes with their feet. They have a look on their faces that could be mistaken for ecstasy.

Then there's a Roman bas-relief of satyrs stomping grapes in a stone basin. The grapes are ankle deep, and two satyrs wrestle playfully with each other while they stomp, dressed not so chastely in what look like jockey shorts. From the mouths of two stone lions the newly trampled vintage pours. Another satyr prepares to pour grapes into the basin. Still another is on a ladder, a rush basket on his back, picking grape clusters from vines clinging to a tree.

One day, as I studied the images in William Younger's classic volume, *Gods, Men, and Wine*, it occurred to me that perhaps no tradition of winemaking captures more for the imagination what it is about than crushing grapes with your feet. For example, there is another picture of an Egyptian hieroglyph showing stompers holding ropes attached to poles overhead so they don't slip. The must is ankle deep, as it is in most of the illustrations from the classical period and earlier. By the Middle Ages, however, the level of the vintage is at least up to the knees and in some cases up to mid-thigh. That's because by then the art of cooperage could provide not only oak barrels but also deep wooden tubs, something not available in the ancient Mediterranean world.

Invariably, the stompers have serene expressions as they pay homage to their god of wine. But there is one picture from an illuminated French manuscript of the fifteenth century in which the grape stomper has an expression on his face of near agony as someone pours more grapes into the wooden tub.

When I saw an advertisement in the local newspaper for Cabernet Franc grapes, I thought of those ancient scenes and I realized what was missing from my education about wine.

I drove to the nearest farm supply store and bought an old-fashioned galvanized washtub that could hold 16¾ gallons. In the laundry room at home, I scoured out the washtub with soap and hot water. I placed it in the middle of the floor in the kitchen and dumped in the grapes. I had washed out a blue plastic bucket and a white enamel washbasin, and filled them with warm water. I found some towels and a clean bath mat in the linen closet.

My son, who was six at the time, was home from school and he found me in the kitchen. He looked perplexed. A confused smile crept across his face, saying, What, are you crazy, Dad?

I rolled up my corduroys to the knees and washed my feet, soaping them up in the white enamel basin. I rinsed them off in the blue bucket. I stood on one foot on the clean bath mat while I dried the other.

Slowly, I lifted my foot and slipped it into the washtub. Cold. The grape clusters had been sitting in the back of my truck overnight, and I wondered if I should have let them warm up to room temperature first. Gary speaks of grapes as if they are sentient beings with their own feelings, and the grapes might have appreciated a bit more warmth. But I couldn't stop now as my foot slid into the tub, crushing the first clusters. I felt a lumpy feeling in the arch and under the ball of my foot, the cold juice squeezing between the toes. I had expected the grapes to feel tepidly warm. But that's a notion I probably picked up from looking at the Roman ceiling mosaic, crushing grapes in warm, sunny Tuscany under an awning to protect oneself from the sun, not in chilly Upstate New York in autumn.

My other foot slid in. The same initial shock of cold. Maybe this is why the medieval treader of grapes had such a look of agony on his face. Perhaps he was from northern France where the autumns are colder. But, similar to the initial splash of jumping into a frigid swimming pool, the discomfort passed as I began to tread. And tread. I felt the skins splitting open and spilling juice and pulp and seeds. I looked down for uncrushed clusters. My big toe searched them out, and when I found them I flattened them. There was a subdued squishing sound as I tread the grapes, and the large lumps subsided slowly into the stew of grape must. Then my feet sought out other clusters and crushed.

My son lingered in the kitchen, watching, perplexed by the ways of fathers.

It took about twenty minutes to crush the grapes so that the lumpiness subsided. And then I was hesitant to stop. I enjoyed the treading. We should make this an annual tradition, I thought, and I felt as if I were a satyr—half animal, half man.

My wife arrived home, and when she saw what I was doing she looked doubtfully at me.

"You crushed them with your feet? Don't expect me to drink it."

I told her that's how they used to do it.

"The old Italian men in my neighborhood never did it that way."

"They did it this way for thousands of years."

"Stay here. I want to get a picture of this." She went to get the camera.

When she returned, the flash popped, and she had a picture. For posterity? A legal proceeding to see if I was of sound mind? She still had the dubious expression.

My son watched silently from a distance, the perplexed look on his brow. I comfort myself: Some day he would understand the ways of men.

My wife suggested I call the wine Eau de Pied, translated as "Foot Water." *Vintage Chateau Eau de Pied.*

Later, I lifted the tub and carried it out to the laundry room. I placed it atop the laundry-folding table. I tore open and added a packet of yeast Gary had provided—it looked and smelled just like the Fleischmann's my wife uses for baking—and I stirred it in with a large wooden spoon. I stretched a cotton towel over the tub and left my wine to take its own course.

Harvest provides its own learning curves. It happened with the Chardonnay one season. A second load had just arrived at the crush pad. Back then, Gary had two small presses. The first press was still pressing and there was only a dribble of juice coming out.

"The problem with white grapes is that you have so much more to press than reds," Gary said. Reds, after they are crushed, ferment with their skins, seeds, and pulp. Only after fermentation are the reds pressed out, and by then many solids have settled and separated from the wine.

When the first press was broken down and cleaned, Gary was expecting more grapes in a half hour. Back then, one wagonload carried enough grapes to fill one press. And there were many more wagons still to come. Gary was gambling on his timing, trying to get the most juice from the must while making sure he was ready with press capacity for the incoming loads.

When Jason, Gary's temporary employee, lifted up the spring-loaded lid to the press, there was a rounded wall about two to three inches thick and three feet tall of rice hulls bloated and damp with grape juice and must debris. He lifted first one, then another of the clamping bars from their slots on the side of the press. The bars held the two curved sides of the barrel-like press together. He unlocked the bars on the opposite side of the press. He reached in and took a clump of hulls in his hand.

"Feels pretty wet to me," Jason said to Gary, who was scouring out a stainless steel bucket.

Jason began to lift off one side of the press, revealing the wall of juice-saturated hulls. Gary came over to check. The wall of hulls began to collapse and he and Jason caught it in their hands before it completely crumbled. That it collapsed under its own weight was one indication that there was still too much juice—and potential wine—in the hulls. The hulls should have been pressed more to squeeze the remaining juice out. The difference would have been a very slightly damp wall of hulls, as opposed to the wet wall we were looking at now.

Gary took it in silently. He was losing juice. He would have to press longer. The tractor would arrive soon with a new load of grapes.

Jason dumped the clumps of rice hulls into a wheelbarrow and pushed it off to the Cabernet Franc vineyard to spread the hulls among the rows.

Joe arrived with the next load from the vineyard. Now the grapes were piling up. The second press was still pressing its first load. Gary checked the pressure. He added more air to bring it up to thirty pounds per square inch, the recommended maximum for that model of press. The trickle of juice didn't increase. Slowly, Gary turned the valve to add more pressure, a few more pounds just to increase the juice run. He stood back, turned, and checked the air pump.

An explosive burst rent the air. A sheet of light green must sprayed toward the wall above the garage door.

Then silence, as everyone stared.

Gary looked for a moment at the green must on the wall.

"Shit," he said. "Goddamn. Shit. Goddamn."

He paced back and forth from the press to the wall, where he took in the damage, a huge spray of splattered light green. The pressure had found a weak spot in the wall of rice hulls where a gap existed between the wooden stays of the press. That's why the recommended air pressure was thirty for that particular press. Gary had been pushing it to thirty-five.

"Shit. Goddamn," Gary repeated. This meant lost production time. He turned off the valve to the press. Everyone stood still, frozen.

The biggest problem was that some of the must—the seeds, skins, and pulp—had landed in the collecting tub where the juice was gathering from the presses. Gary had to stop the juice pumping from the tub to one of the stainless steel tanks. He had to stop solids from getting into the tank. He switched off the pump.

"Disconnect the hose to the tank," he told John Chandler.

"The juice will have to be rescreened," John said as he pulled one of the clamps that held the hose to the collection tub. The slurry of must floated in the juice.

Jason walked in. He didn't know what had happened because as he walked in through the garage door he didn't see the spray of green must above the door behind him. But he saw that the hose had been disconnected from the holding tank. Then he turned around.

"Uh . . . oh. Something happened."

Then Joe was there and he looked around. He saw the wall and the back of the overhead door. "Looks like a little accident."

Gary grinned. "I thought it could take more pressure," he said.

They cleaned up. They sprayed the walls with hot water before the juice dried and the must adhered. Gary began screening the juice in the collecting tub to remove any solids. But he couldn't rule out that some got sucked into the tank.

"It's going to be chunky Chardonnay. The only one of its kind. Chunky Chardonnay. I like that," he said.

And in his imagination he envisioned a label announcing: "Chunky Chardonnay."

That's when he vowed to buy a better press . . . and a better crusher . . . and . . .

In 2005 he did buy a bigger press, made in Slovenia, for $28,000. His old press could press 1,200 to 1,400 pounds of fermented red grapes per hour, while the new one could press five tons per hour. The next year he bought a bigger crusher-destemmer, an Italian Laguna that could process five tons of grapes an hour, as opposed to his old one that could do only three tons an hour. The Laguna cost $11,000. This led to the bigger 5,000-liter stainless steel tank with a refrigeration jacket: $11,000. The Bobcat tractor cost $30,000. But it took the steering on the old tractor to fail to persuade him to buy the new one.

This accounts in part for why Gary and Rosie's investment in the winery is now pushing $1 million. Then there have been other expenses. The price of French oak barrels increased 80 percent because of the rise in the value of the euro in recent years. And they purchased adjacent cleared land—sixty-two acres—when it came available.

"I didn't want anyone putting up something that would ruin the view," Gary said.

And in his worst nightmares he could imagine golden arches with the lake as a bucolic backdrop.

At least in principle, making wine is straightforward.

Fermentation will begin when the grapes are crushed because grapes have their own natural yeast blooms on the skins. But after crushing the Riesling, Gary waited several days, intentionally restraining the fermentation by denying the juice air until more solids settled out. Then he racked it—removed the solids—twice, pumping the juice into another tank to settle some more, and then into still another. Each transfer left solids at the bottom of the tank that were drained out. On the smaller tanks he placed the stainless steel lid at wine level and inflated the O ring to keep out air and to hold down fermentation until he was ready.

Finally, he pumped the Riesling back into the tall tank and prepared to add yeast to jump-start fermentation.

In his lab, a small room no larger than a moderately sized kitchen with a double stainless steel sink, a counter for testing, and a pharmacist's triple-beam scales, he took from a box a paper package of Go-ferm, a nutrient that feeds yeast, and placed it on the counter. He opened a cabinet and pulled out packages of yeast strains cultivated for fermenting grapes. He placed them next to the Go-ferm on the counter.

Out by the garage door he scoured out a couple of white plastic buckets with the hot water hose. A late autumn afternoon came on as a long line of cirrus clouds, wisps and tufts reaching upward toward the blue, began to present a spectacular range of colors—pink, salmon, blood red, and purple—that appeared as ribbons as the light of the lowering sun was refracted.

Gary sat down at his makeshift desk in the winery and began recording the volume of must for the Riesling and the multipliers for the yeast. He poked at the keys of a digital calculator to determine how much yeast he would need. Then he calculated how much he would need in nutrients to get the yeast on a fast track.

It's a time for caution. There was the year he went through the same exercise, and when he had finished with the calculations, he sat back in the oak office chair, looking at them quizzically. "Is that right?" he muttered to himself. He scanned the figures, and he looked tired. It was one of those moments when the fatigue of the harvest season had set in. He was so distracted that he had done the calculations mechanically without thinking about what he was really trying to accomplish. That's dangerous, he knew, and he could ruin an entire vintage that way. So he started over on the calculations, punching in the volume, and the multiplier for the yeast, and the one for the nutrient Go-ferm. When he finished, he looked at the calculation. Now he knew he had it right.

That was a lesson then, and that was why he was overly cautious now as he prepared to add yeast to his precious first Riesling crop. Finishing the calculation, he returned to the lab and measured out the powdery nutrient for the yeast on a white paper plate atop the apothecary scales. He was precise, adding a little more with a large stainless steel table spoon, taking a little away, then adding a little more. He placed one of the white plastic buckets in the sink and turned on both the hot and cold water taps. He put his fingers in the flow, adjusted the tap to an approximate temperature, then began to fill the bucket. As it filled, he placed a foot-long thermometer in the bucket. He adjusted the water temperature. He needed 110 degrees Fahrenheit. He took the thermometer out, shook it, then added some more cold water. Finally, he had the temperature right.

He poured the paper plate of nutrient into the warm water. He stirred with a tablespoon and the water slowly turned into a brown viscous broth. He mixed the second batch of nutrient in the other bucket. Next, he measured out the brown, powdery yeast on the paper plate. It had a slightly sour smell very much like conventional baking yeast. When the temperature in the white buckets had declined to 104 degrees Fahrenheit, he poured the yeast into them and began stirring.

"Now we have to wait for about fifteen minutes."

That's because not only must the yeast rise but the temperature of the mix must come down so it's within eighteen degrees of the wine's temperature. Otherwise the shock could kill the yeast.

We stepped out of the lab.

"Want a glass a wine?"

He poured each of us a glass of Zinfandel from his '98 vintage, his last year as a hobbyist winemaker and vinted with grapes he had shipped from California. "This is good."

We nursed the wine. While we drank he stepped outside under the porch of the crush pad. "Come see the sunset," he said.

I stepped outside and looked west. There was a brilliant display of the same colors I saw earlier but more luminescent, almost blinding now, as the setting sun's rays played off the underside of the clouds.

Gary held his glass up after taking a sip, toasting the declining sun.

We returned to the yeast. It had risen and looked like a brown cake in each of the containers. Gary took one bucket and walked over to a valve on the tall stainless steel tank. He placed the pail under the valve, turned it on, and the juice flowed.

"That's so the yeast won't be too shocked," he said, explaining the reason for diluting the yeast first.

He stirred the combination. He checked the temperature. He waited.

"One of the most critical things is temperature," he said.

He checked it once more. Finally, with one of the white buckets in hand, he climbed an aluminum ladder up to the top of the tall stainless steel tank. He raised a round door on the top, tilted the pail, and poured in the yeast. You could hear it hit the juice in the tank. He carried the second white bucket up the ladder and did the same. Then he connected the hose from the bottom of the tank to the wine pump, and then one from the wine pump up to the top of the tank. He turned on the pump and began pumping wine and yeast from the bottom up and over the top of the tank to mix the two.

The conversion of sugar to alcohol is probably the most fundamental and earliest form of organic energy production for sustaining life, going back some four billion years, according to Patrick E. McGovern, an internationally recognized biomolecular archaeologist at the University of Pennsylvania. While wine grapes do have sufficient natural yeast to ferment on their own, they can be unpredictable. So man inserts himself into the process and has introduced yeast strains with a proven record.

Yeast is a single-cell, plant-like fungus that occurs naturally in nature. A microorganism with a voluptuous oblong shape, the cell is so small that it would take twenty billion cells to weigh one gram, or one/twenty-eighth of an ounce. But, if yeast cells are infinitesimally small, they have giant appetites. In one hour one yeast cell can convert the equivalent of its body weight in sugar to alcohol. Imagine a 150-pound person eating 150 pounds of Big Macs and converting it in an hour into . . . fertilizer.

Fleischmann's can take one yeast cell and propagate it to produce 60,000 gallons of what's called wet yeast or cream yeast. (Fleischmann's would invent dry yeast, the kind most home bakers use now, during World War II so fresh bread could be baked in the field for American GIs.) The baking yeast strain is basically the same as the one used by Gary for his wine. Called *Saccharomyces cerevisiae*, it is the basis for all yeasts used in baking and fermenting. *Cerevisiae* means brewer, and one detects its equivalent in *cerveza*, the Spanish word for beer.

The proven record of *Saccharomyces cerevisiae* is one of some antiquity. According to wine residue such as seeds and skins found in wine jars more than five thousand years old from ancient Egypt, the same basic yeast strain is also used by Betty Crocker. But here is what remains curious: While *Saccharomyces cerevisiae* occurs naturally as blooms on the surface of grapes, perhaps transported by bees, it does not occur naturally on grains or vegetables, according to a study of the yeast's DNA.

The implication is clear, according to McGovern, who has taken the lead in establishing the earliest origins of wine through chemical analysis with an infrared spectrometer of the grape residues in ancient wine jars and on potsherds: "Neither bread nor beer came first . . . but a sugar-rich material." In all likelihood that sugar-rich material was grapes.

Dates, figs, and honey can also harbor the yeast strain, which accounts for why the ancients also made date, fig, and honey wines. But unlike grape wine, water has to be added to those concoctions. "Grapes, when their juices have been exuded, provide the ideal breeding ground for the yeast to multiply and convert sugars into alcohol. The must has just the right amount of water and nutrient mix, so it does not require dilution as do sugar-rich honey and the juices of more fibrous fruits," McGovern writes. Moreover, the natural suitability of wine grapes for this purpose helps to account for why more than 3,500 years ago the Hittites, in what is today modern Turkey, had beer-wine—they added grapes to make the grain and water ferment. The same with the Sumerians nearly 4,000 years ago. The yeasts used by bakers and brewers today had, in all likelihood, their origins thousands of years ago in the fermenting of wine.

The Anchor Steam Beer Company, the well-known brewery in San Francisco, discovered in 2002 just how important yeast from grapes was when it took the oldest surviving recipe for brewing beer contained in the nearly four-thousand-year-old Sumerian poem "Hymn to Ninkasi" and attempted to duplicate it as a commercial beverage. Among the lines that challenged the brewers at Anchor was the one that called for "brewing it with honey and wine." To both the beer drinker and the enophile, such a mix is likely unappetizing. But there was a method to what the early beer makers in Sumer were trying to do, a method that had been lost. Because on further investigation, and with the assistance of the original translator of the hymn (the hymn was not translated until 1964), the Sumerian word for wine was also the same word for grapes.

Wine, then, came first and made both bread and beer possible. There is another consequence. By adding grapes, or crushed grapes, to their brew, the ancient Sumerians were engaged in a ritual that subsequent generations of bakers, brewers, and vintners—such as Gary—would re-enact, adding an outside source of yeast to jump-start fermentation.

And if you don't get the yeast right, the result can be disaster. Gary recalled it happened to him one time when he was making Grenache. Fermentation on the wine had already started from the natural yeast blooms on the grapes. But Gary thought it had not progressed far and added yeast anyway.

"It started foaming. It was coagulating with a pink foam."

The fall when I stomped grapes and tried to make my own wine at home, I observed the ways of yeast. A couple of days after I had mixed the yeast into the tub of crushed grapes, I began to detect occasional telltale bubbles on the surface of the mixture. By the fourth day, the stew of dark red must was in full fermentation, and I could see large bubbles of carbon dioxide rise slowly to the surface, bubbling up, under, around, and over the half-submerged skins of the grapes.

If I had any doubts that the wine was fermenting, they were dispelled the next day when I returned home and smelled that distinctive perfume. It's the smell that McGovern observed attracted animals in the wild to wild grapes fermenting on the vine: "Organisms as different as the fruit fly and the elephant gravitate to fermented fruits, and they have similar physiological responses. In the most general sense, their predilections are understandable because sugar fermentation is the earliest form of energy production for sustaining life. . . . The ethanol production is like a signal sent up to the sugar lovers of the world, since this pungent, volatile compound leads back to a source of glucose or fructose." Birds in particular are attracted to fermenting grapes on the vine, and have been observed to get drunk, or what McGovern describes as "ensuing uncoordinated muscular movements." Then he adds parenthetically, "(robins have been known to fall off their perches)." All of this, from the delights of fermenting grapes on the vine.

What I was responding to then was the age-old olfactory allure locked up in my genes. It was indeed a delicious smell.

I had planned to wait a full week for the fermentation to take place. But on the evening of the fifth day the bubbles had slowed down. On the morning of the sixth there were no more little burps giving off carbon dioxide.

I tasted the wine. It was alcoholic, but it also had a very faint smell of hydrogen sulfide—rotten eggs.

The next step was to press out the wine. But I did not own a press. So, Gary recommended a method he had used in the past: pantyhose. According to him, pantyhose provide an excellent means for squeezing wine out of the must.

"I know. It sounds weird," he said one evening as he filled our glasses from one of the barrels with a tasting. "I mean, you have the feeling that people are looking at you kind of strange when you buy them. Because you have to buy the biggest size you can find. Four X. You can squeeze more out of them."

I bet, I thought. And I reinforced myself with a larger than normal gulp of wine.

"Go to a dollar store. They're the cheapest."

I went to a dollar store in Cortland and found a transitional Triple X–Four X that apparently fit both categories of Xs.

Back home, I ripped open the plastic packaging and took out the pantyhose. I looked them over and wondered, should I wash them in advance? No, too much effort. I decided to tie the legs in knots at the top of the thighs. Then I wouldn't have to worry about flopping appendages.

I washed out the white enamel pan. I would squeeze the wine into it. I also had a Carlo Rossi gallon-wine jug Gary had loaned me. When he was an amateur winemaker he used them for transfers of small quantities to barrels, and he still used them, although the irony did not pass unnoticed. Gary, a lover of fine wine, had somehow acquired Carlo Rossi jug wine bottles, and Carlo Rossi, made by Gallo, is the largest-selling jug wine in the country.

"Friends and relatives gave them to me," he said, and insisted, "*I* never drank Carlo Rossi."

I held the pantyhose at the waistband over the galvanized fermentation tub. With one of my wife's cooking pots I scooped up the fermented must and used the bottom edge to stretch open the waistband. I tilted the pot and poured the must into the pantyhose. I took another scoop and poured. The pantyhose were reasonably filled. I clasped the waistband in one hand and tightened my grip around it. I grasped the knots I had tied in the upper legs and swiftly lifted the pantyhose from the galvanized tub to the white basin, wine dribbling on the top of the washing machine.

I began twisting the pantyhose, wringing it like a towel, tighter and tighter, over the enamel pan. The juice flowed out as I twisted. When I could twist no more, I released my grip on the waistband. The must was still damp, more damp than if it had been pressed in a wine press. I clamped the waistband closed and twisted once more. But I could squeeze out only a couple of drops. I released the waistband and dumped the must into a garbage can.

I poured more must into the pantyhose and did the same thing. Every time I transferred from the galvanized tub to the white enamel pan I lost a little wine, much of which went down into the washing machine. Later, I added some detergent, set the washing machine on a large load, and washed on a normal cycle in cold water. I also washed out my wife's pot. She never knew the difference.

In the end, I filled the Carlo Rossi gallon jug, and one and a half three-quarter liter wine bottles. I sealed the containers.

"You're weird," my wife said when I told her I had pressed out the wine with pantyhose.

"But Gary told me to do it."

"He's weird."

And all for nothing. The wine went bad—the rotten egg smell only got worse. Even though Gary tried to fix it, the smell wouldn't go away.

"You could use it for salad dressing," he offered.

I dumped it. We were never sure why it went bad, but later I read that you shouldn't make wine in galvanized steel. A chemical reaction?

Different varieties of grapes are picked at different times depending on their maturity. The year the Riesling were picked, the Chardonnay were picked a week later. That time Gary could get only two Mexican pickers. So he and Dan joined in the harvesting. "It was the day from hell," he said. The pickers didn't finish until dusk. That night Gary got to bed at 1 a.m. and was up at 4:45 a.m.

He picked the Cabernet Franc a week after that, in the beginning of November. This time he got three of the Mexican pickers, with Levi and Dan helping out.

Some years Gary ferments the Chardonnay in one of the stainless steel tanks and other years he does it in the barrels. When using the barrels, he fills them three-quarters full so plenty of air is available for fermentation. Next, he adds yeast to each barrel, then stirs. He replaces the cork, leaving it loose so air can continue to pass through to feed the fermentation, and carbon dioxide can escape. A few days later, if you pulled a bung from one of the barrels of Chardonnay and put your ear down to the bung hole, you could hear the little yeast creatures within burbling and burping.

Because the Cabernet Franc are red, they are processed differently.

Instead of being pumped to the press after crushing like the whites are, the juice, pulp, and skins of reds are pumped into food-grade 250-gallon plastic tubs. They are fermented with the skins because that's how red wines get their red color. Once the yeast is added, the tubs are covered loosely with plastic and the fermentation usually takes about a week. Again, the telltale bubbles of carbon dioxide rise to the surface.

When all was done the year Gary made his first Riesling from his own crop, he ended up with 900 gallons of the vintage. He also had 486 gallons of newly vinted Cabernet Franc, 380 gallons of Chardonnay, and 250 gallons of Pinot Gris. ("It's just beautiful," he said.)

"It was a tough growing year. It was real wet. It was sixteen to eighteen growing days below normal. So the harvest is not too bad," Gary said. "Dan really did a good job."

And eventually, when the Riesling was bottled the following spring, Gary was not disappointed. "It's good. It's the first crop. And it's only going to get better."

When I tasted it, it was earthy, or as Gary characterized it, it had some minerality. He also said it had some peach, but that I struggled with.

The unexpected winner, however, here in Rieslingland, was the Pinot Gris. It was the first time Gary had made Pinot Gris. When I tasted, it was full bodied and you could appreciate the citrus, especially pineapple. Gary said there was melon. That I didn't get—again, perhaps it was a difference in our palates. But there was no doubt for

a first harvest he had reason to be pleased. If the grapes were "just beautiful," as he described them during harvest, the wine when bottled turned out to be "better than beautiful. The fermentation aromas were just as they are now. If I were going to grow more grapes, I would plant Pinot Gris."

So once again, the land was exerting its influence, making and reshaping him in its own image, in a manner of speaking. "The only question is, will I ever be able to make a Pinot Gris like this again?"

There are times when the winemaker does make the perfect wine.

That was the case with Gary's first Cabernet Franc harvest. And that changed his mind about the prospects for the varietal that had been haunting him since he planted it—that there wasn't enough of a market for the lesser known Cab Franc. When he bottled it he knew it was a winner. So what if it didn't actually win a prize, he thought at the time. But it did.

That first Cab Franc crop was Joe's glory. "The growing conditions were perfect," Gary said of the vintage. "It was a hot summer. We had less than two tons per acre."

It was a small crop because it was the first crop. The young vines had naturally, because of their youth, undercropped—like a teenage stripling who is suddenly becoming a man but doesn't yet have the heft to go with the growth. Gary could not have asked for a better crop.

He sensed it would be a promising wine when he smelled the aroma of the grapes being crushed. He would pause while dumping grapes into the crusher and breathe in the headiness of the fruit. Rich aromas, he thought. And the color: fabulous, rich.

The wine fermented for the next week. Gary used the yeast strain CSM. The particular yeast strain can make the difference to the particular grape varietal. "It especially helps to take away that green bell pepper taste that you find in Cabernet Franc," he said.

After inoculating the crushed grapes with yeast, Gary began to sense fermenting aromas a couple days later. By the third day, he said, "I knew this was going to be a good wine." And having a good Cab Franc was doubly exciting because he was producing his own wine with *his own* grapes.

This has nice body, he thought when the fermentation was complete and he tasted the wine. It was young, of course, in the way of nouveau wines, such as Beaujolais which is shipped from Burgundy to thirsty fans in November as a fresh, unaged wine—something to anticipate with winter arriving. In the case of the Cabernet Franc this meant that it was astringent or tart when he tasted it. Those qualities overwhelmed the potential of the tastes he would find once the wine aged. It lacked the fullness and complexity he would expect of a mature red as well as flavor compounds that were yet to emerge.

The wine went through malolactic fermentation, converting the harsh malic acid into lactic acid, and more mature flavors asserted themselves. They weren't there yet, but Gary knew they would emerge. Every couple of weeks he topped off the barrels as the ML worked slowly through its cycle.

The fruit is really coming out, Gary thought, when malolactic fermentation finished in December. He took drops from each barrel, and applied them to paper chromatography, which indicates the progress of the ML fermentation through color. The samples turned blue, meaning the conversion to lactic acid had completed.

There's a nice texture, Gary thought as he tasted. The mouthfeel had round full flavors and he was a little surprised because it hadn't been aged for any length of time in a barrel. Despite that, it was more full-bodied by the end of the malolactic fermentation. And that was a harbinger of things to come.

"The color was rich, garnet, dark ruby," Gary said. In other words, it wasn't something you expected from such a young wine.

Gary hit it with sulfur dioxide to preserve it and kill residual bacteria that could remain active and could spoil the wine. The sulfur dioxide assured that it would be more stable. Sulfur dioxide, which is ubiquitous and necessary in wine, is a major reason you see on the back of wine labels "Contains sulfites," to which a small number of people are allergic. In addition, trace amounts of sulfur are added when barrels are sterilized. And of course sulfur is used in the vineyard to contain diseases of the vine. The devil's measure is wine's bosom friend.

Several weeks later the tannins were receding. He characterized it as the tannins "lying down"—in a sense going to sleep. Again, there was a little more fruit. And the oak was beginning to assert itself.

Two months later: Wow. Cranberry. Not strong. But it was there. The wine was marrying well with the oak. The oak was bringing out the aromas. He bottled the following August, and in the fall he entered the wine in the American Wine Society competition.

It was a late evening in November when he arrived home in Cortland from the winery keen on checking the competition results. A cold, wet autumn night was settling in on the street where Rosie and Gary live. In the headlights of his truck the streets reflected wet and slick.

"I'm going to check the Wine Society site," he told Rosie as he went up to her second-floor office at home. He wanted to see who the winners were. Not that he would get his hopes up. At least not consciously. But there was always that secret hope. He knew it was a winning vintage. But winning depends as much on the palates of individual judges as on the wine. In the end, despite the best intentions of judges, it depended on their frame of mind and all the contingencies of daily life that made it difficult to steer a middle, balanced course. Gary knew this so he said he wouldn't get his hopes up.

The website was slow to appear, probably because so many other wine aficionados were also trying to access the results of the competition. Finally, on the home page he scrolled down to the link "Wine Competition." That took him to the page "Commercial Wine Competition Results."

He was hoping for a silver but would accept a bronze. He just wanted to know that he could make a wine that the gurus of wine judgment would appreciate. Any affirmation, even a bronze, would justify what he did.

Gary scrolled down past "Eagle Crest, *New York*, 2005, Diamond, Silver," "Gray Ghost Vineyards, *Virginia*, 2004, Cabernet Sauvignon, Bronze."

He continued and reached "Lake Chelan Winery," the first of the L's on the screen.

In his haste, Gary scrolled beyond the Ls. He arrived at the M's. There was a long list for Magnotta Winery, *Ontario*, a dozen awards.

He returned to the L's but scrolled down slowly now. "Let's see what we've got," he said.

He found Little Hills Winery, *Missouri*, NV, Chardonel, Bronze.

Finally, he arrived at Long Point: "Long Point Winery, *New York*, 2005, Cabernet Franc, Gold."

He looked at it for a moment. "Gold." Gold. And then it registered.

He walked downstairs to tell Rosie.

"Hey Ro, we won a gold medal for our Cab Franc."

"No, you didn't."

"Yes, we did."

"Come on."

"We did."

She went up to look for herself. Gary followed.

"That's great!" she said. "See, you can make gold medal wines from grapes grown in New York."

Gary had long lamented the challenges.

"That was Joe's year right there," he said.

Gary had a new respect for the grape that made the wine. It was a perfect wine. All 118 cases. A half year later it had sold out.

But then the letdown hit: Would he ever make the perfect Cabernet Franc again? Would the land let him? Then he began to doubt himself, and said, "There's no such thing as perfection."

It was my wife's idea to do a wine tasting. That's when I learned to spit.

We were in Ithaca on a Saturday afternoon in November. It was a sunny, bitterly cold day in whose chill the sunshine was a reminder of the coming winter. When we had finished our errands, she said, "Aren't there some wineries nearby?"

"Not far."

"Maybe we should do a wine tasting?"

"I like that idea."

Already, in my mind I was making plans to expand our itinerary.

We headed north on Route 89, hugging the west shore of Cayuga Lake, and there was a wonderful feeling of escape on a Saturday afternoon, forgetting about the laundry, the repairs on the house, shopping. We would avoid one winery, because they had a reputation for catering to the party crowd. If we could get that far, I wanted to go to a winery Gary recommended.

At our first winery, we drove around a bend of bushes on a gravel lane and were met by a modest, single-story ranch house. It was a reminder of just how much the making of wine is as much a smallholder's occupation. Not unlike many of the small wineries on the Cote de Or in Burgundy: one-man operations, with the wife and kids pitching in.

The tasting room was cozy. Windows and glass doors on the backside looked out on a wide deck with tables and chairs and a perch from which to take in the chill blue of Cayuga Lake reflecting the cold blue of the sky.

I started with the Chardonnay. I took a large gulp, enough to fill my mouth so that I could get the full effect. I think that was one of my initial problems in learning wine tasting, taking sips that were too gingerly. You need to take enough into the mouth to really taste the wine.

I absorbed the taste. Not bad, I thought as I looked at the lake in the distance. I could tell the Chardonnay was not as heavily oaked as Gary's. To my surprise, I liked that. But it was a bit tart. Still, not bad. I tried another white, I don't remember which one, and for me it was not memorable. Then I tried a semi-dry Riesling. My reaction was immediate: too sweet.

That's when I did something I had never done before. I spit it back in my glass. And I did it unconsciously. I realized, why swallow what you don't like?

Next came the reds.

I tried a hybrid, Chambourcin. Again, not bad. It had more body than I expected, perhaps only slightly less so than the *Vitis vinifera* varietals I was familiar with. And perhaps not quite as lively to the tastebuds in my mouth, but again, only a little less so.

However, I still had difficulty distinguishing the subtleties of different tastes. Some days I'm good at it. Other days I'm not. Maybe it has something to do with what I eat for lunch.

I tried the Cab Franc next. I had high hopes for it, given that it was *Vitis vinifera*. It was different. "Smoky," I blurted out. I turned to my wife. "Smoky." But once again it had less oak than Gary's, and that intrigued me.

Then the last red, and I can't remember what it was, but once again I involuntarily spit. I didn't like what it did to my palate, and I found myself missing, of all things, the Chambourcin. I can't say why, but I didn't appreciate the aftertaste of the last red.

"Are there any you liked enough that you would want me to buy?" I asked my wife.

"I don't know."

At this point, the wine pourer retreated to a corner of the room behind the tasting corner so we could confer. Of course, if he were a true salesman he would have stayed at the counter to shame us with his presence. Instead he was very civil about it.

"You like Cab Franc. Did you like this one?" I asked.

"I don't know. I don't know if I like it enough."

"I agree. I thought maybe it was a little too smoky. How about the Chambourcin?"

"It was okay."

"I liked it. Let's get a bottle. And even though I don't care much for Chardonnay, I want to get a bottle. We can save it for summer. Or when we have guests who enjoy whites. I like that it has less oak."

In the end, I bought the Cab Franc anyway. I was intrigued by the smoke.

"Shall we try another winery?" I said as we returned to the car.

"Sure, why not," my wife said. "Shall we try ... ?"

"We've been there. I would like to try something new. There's one Gary thinks a lot of."

"Okay."

As we drove along the lake, it kept coming back to me: I spat. I didn't even think about it when I did it. Spitting, of course, is important for professional winetasters because they often have to taste many different wines at a sitting and they must stay sober.

Anyway, I spat because I didn't care for the wine. And there was something else. I had avoided spitting before because if I didn't swallow, I didn't get to taste the wine in the back of my mouth. But this time I permitted just a minute amount into the back of my gullet to taste it with those taste buds on the back of the tongue. And it seemed enough to tell me if it was any better at the back of my mouth than at the front.

So that's how it's done, I thought.

Not only that, but I was enjoying tasting. I was enjoying attempting to tease meaning from the wine. I didn't feel I was pretending to taste, as I had many times before when I was first learning how to taste.

The tasting room at the next winery was in a converted post-and-beam barn.

I tasted the Chardonnay, and spat. I tasted a Vidal Blanc, and spat. I tasted a Cab Franc, and swallowed. But it seemed light and emaciated, without body, an old nag ready for the knacker. Then I tasted an inexpensive non-vintage red, made with Cab Franc and a slight amount of white added to give a little residual sugar. Maybe that gives the illusion of a little more softness, I thought as the wine pourer poured.

I tasted. Again, my judgment was tentative—not bad. I was waiting for it to sink in so that I could define what it was about this wine that I enjoyed. Then it occurred to me that it was good. I liked it more than the *vinifera* varietals.

I bought two bottles, and later when we drank them, my wife and I both agreed, "pretty good" for an inexpensive bottle of wine.

We stopped at another winery. I was on a roll. In front of a fireplace, warmed by the flames, I tasted several wines. A couple I tasted again. I liked them enough. But while I thought I was being judicious, I was not. Because later, after I bought two bottles and opened them, I said to myself that I would rather drink Gary's Moon Pooch. And I recalled an admonition he once gave me: If you do too many tastings you can lose the ability to discriminate. "After a while, it can all taste like motor oil."

On the drive around the north end of the lake, my wife suggested, "Why don't we eat at the Aurora Inn? I'll treat."

We arrived a little after 5 p.m. at the nineteenth-century brick inn with the big two-story portico. It was already dark and the carriage lamps beckoned us into the reception anteroom, on one side of which a gas fire in a fireplace wavered and danced. The *maître d'* showed us a table in the dining room, where the flames of two more gas fireplaces did sprightly dance. There we ordered pot roast for a cold night.

But the wine proved even better.

"What would you like to drink?" the waitress asked.

"Honey?" I asked my wife.

"What do you think?"

"It's a cold night. I would like a Cab. Your house." I said.

"I'll have the same," my wife said.

"By the way, what is your house wine?"

"Long Point."

"Wonderful," both of us said in unison. We smiled, already feeling in our imaginations the warm glow of something familiar.

The waitress brought the wine, and it was rich and dark. In the flickering light of the fire it had wonderful "legs," the rivulets of wine that cling to the edge of the glass. It was an ideal wine for a cold night. And we both agreed that it was the best pot roast we ever ate—even better than mine. Smugly, we both agreed that the wine was the best we had that day.

Later, at about seven o'clock, we drove past Long Point Winery on the way home. It was dark, except for a couple of outside overhead lights illuminating the building on a frigid Saturday night. Gary, undoubtedly, was at home with Rosie, playing with the grandkids.

By November, another season's wine has been made. That is reason enough to celebrate the harvest and vintage. The nature of Upstate in late autumn, cold and damp, provided another reason to celebrate indoors with wine and food.

On a bitterly cold and blustery Sunday afternoon as the sun sank below the horizon, the dusk spread over the broad rolling fields of the Canadian Shield that stretched into the dark. The color had drained from the land into the black lake.

Inside the winery the sound of a woman's laughter rippled above the conversation, slipping among the tawny wine barrels like some fluttering wraith. On the balcony up by the offices that overlooked the lines of oak barrels and the diners at their tables, an old accordionist rocked from side to side as his fingers played up and down the white and black keys. His face was pasty, sagging with age, and he sang "Amore" in a gruff baritone. Next to him, a more slender septuagenarian picked at his electrified mandolin, providing a sprightly harmony and plucked syncopation.

The woman's laughter echoed again and a flash of red silk scarf slipped among the waitresses.

"I hope you don't mind sitting here," Rosie said, as she seated a couple who had just arrived, a graying college professor with a robust stomach and the kind of curvy, blond wife that mean-spirited gossipers might characterize as a trophy. They were not talking to each other.

Rosie then was off to seat another couple.

It was Gary and Rosie's annual Italian harvest fest at Long Point. And it represented many things in the annual cycle. Most obviously, the gathering represented the end of the harvest and the beginning of the new vintage, just as it did in Italy—and in France, Spain, Germany, and anywhere the harvest is celebrated. And it was another means of marketing a small winery, an attempt by Gary and Rosie to get the word out by throwing an extravaganza in which diners ate chicken tetrazzini or eggplant parmigiana and drank eight different wines Gary had vinted. But, in the bleakness of November in Upstate New York, the fest was also a protest against the coming winter, the winery providing a welcome illusion of Adriatic sunshine and warmth.

A busload arrived from Syracuse, organized by one of Gary's friends. Some were from the old Italian neighborhood. Others were just looking for an opportunity to resist the cold November gray by making an outing to the shores of Cayuga Lake.

They sold sixty-two tickets for the four o'clock seating—they'd also had a seating at two o'clock—and Gary now wandered amid the crowd shaking hands with old friends, welcoming new potential customers, and generally playing the *signore* welcoming with outspread arms the Americans to his estate.

"There are people here who know too much about me," he said with a grin as he greeted some new arrivals.

The duo on the balcony now played "Lara's Theme" from
Dr. Zhivago, which on the accordion didn't sound very much Russian
but voluptuous Italian instead. The rough baritone continued his gentle rocking from side to side—he could have been playing in a taverna
on the coast of Abruzzi. One could sense that when his generation
was gone, the music would go with them: The children of the children
of the old generation have better things to do than listen to memories
of the *patria*. They've got their timeshares and their wide screens and
their Jacuzzis and sports cars. And so the old music, played by old
men, will fade away.

Gary introduced the diners to the estate Chardonnay. "This was
barrel fermented. I chose it because it would be light on the palate and
go well with the antipasto."

The antipasto arrived, plates of salad, green, brown and black olives
unpitted, and salami, bruschetta, and coils of dark red prosciutto.

"This is a very good Chardonnay," said Rich, a teacher from Syracuse. "I tried his other two Chardonnays and they didn't do anything
for me. But this one," he said, holding the glass to his nose as he drew
in the aroma, "this one is very good. I bought a case."

One more vindication for Gary.

"Yes, I would say it's slightly buttery," he said to his neighbor, the
college professor. "But I've had Chardonnays that were much more
buttery. And in France they can really be quite sharp."

The college professor spit out a brown olive pit on to the tines of his
fork and nodded agreeably.

The duo now played "O Sole Mio," and the coarseness of the baritone took it from Caruso's opera stage and returned it to its origins,
some Neapolitan back street, narrow and cobblestoned and festooned
with colorful laundry hanging from lines. The red scarf flashed, flow-
ing between the heads of waitresses. It belonged to a well-tanned
blonde. Did some guests fly in from Florida?

The entrees arrived along with more wine. Later, for dessert, they
had Italian-style cheesecake baked by Rosemary's mother.

"Both are barrel-aged," Gary said, as he described the attributes
of his dessert wines, his voice seeking to emerge from the buzz of
conversation.

"He's right. Good fruit," one diner said. The power of suggestion.

But not everyone was happy. One man, who drank liberally, told his wife loudly—looking for attention—"They're going to change the wine, aren't they? I've had enough of that shit."

Gary gave a little speech. He stood against the oak barrels stacked three high. And all of a sudden there was another Gary. He was no longer the in-your-face, street-smart, Northside kid who had donned the imperial purple. Instead, he sounded vulnerable and not quite at ease. Perhaps because it was hard to hear his voice on the opposite side of the room. He stood, his head just above the heads of the seated diners, and he spoke in an almost gentle, plaintive tone.

"Is everybody having a good time?"

"Yeah," came sporadic voices.

"Is everybody having a good time?" he asked, a bit louder.

"Yes," sounded a fuller chorus.

"I want to thank all of you for coming out this evening. I know you're enjoying the meal."

But you could just barely make out what he's saying. Gary has the kind of voice that blends with the buzz of others in a warm gentle static. You saw his moving lips above the heads of diners. Some attempted to listen. Others continued their own buzz with their neighbors. As Gary's lips moved over the heads of the diners, he looked strangely disembodied. And then you realized that all this Irish-Italian kid wanted to do is make wine, not peddle it.

Now Rosemary got up. How different. She has a rich, commanding contralto that cut swiftly through the buzz: It was the antidote to the diners' distraction as her voice effortlessly called for attention and heads turned.

"This morning Gary said, 'I'll never do this again.' But after tonight I know he'll say, 'This is the best event we've ever had.'"

There were several cheers. Rosemary thanked the performers and Fabio, an Italian restaurateur from Cortland who prepared the meal. She thanked Gary for the husband that he was. And then her voice began to quaver.

"Every year Gary's mother has helped. This is the first year she couldn't be with us." That's because amid everything else, working two jobs, making and selling the wine, the birth of a grandchild, Gary's mother was now in the nursing home. Rosie paused, trying to regain

control, but her voice continued to tremble. "And I just want to re-member her because she's such a wonderful woman."

There were cheers and applause. In Rosie's voice could be detected the weariness of the last year. All of a sudden it's all there in her voice, as well as the love for someone who is consumed by a desire to make the perfect wine in an imperfect land.

Old friends started clamoring. "Kiss her. Kiss her, Gary. A kiss. A kiss."

The diners joined the chorus.

"A kiss. A kiss."

Gary, who stood next to Rosie, hesitated for a moment, then turned and gave her a light kiss on the lips.

"Nah, a real kiss, Gary," someone cried out.

"A real kiss. A kiss," the audience demanded, and Caesar was being judged in the arena by his own.

Gary hesitated, and what emerged was his shy side, one not prone to displays of public emotion. It must've been the Irish in him, his ear still echoing with Father O'Reilly's admonitions against public passion.

"A real kiss," the chorus demanded, like at a gladiatorial fete, thumbs outthrust in one hand while quaffing from a bowl of the best Falernian in the other.

A shy grin spread on Gary's face. Finally, he turned, firmly put both hands on Rosemary's shoulders, and pulled her close to him. They were superimposed against the tawny oak barrels. And then, reenacting in its briefest outlines what must long have been an ancient ritual in many a wine cellar, Gary turned his head and planted a long, passionate kiss on Rosie's lips.

He lingered, then pulled away.

The audience erupted in loud applause amid a couple of cries of "Go for it, Gary." The thumbs were upraised. The vintage had been celebrated.

So the seasons come full circle. At the end of November and into December it's cleanup time in the vineyard, removing dead vines, doing some light pruning, hilling up, spreading potash, replacing broken posts. Some years the vineyardist gets lucky because the weather turns unexpectedly mild. One day it was almost balmy, if temperatures in the mid-fifties can be considered balmy. The weather provided a calming accompaniment to the decline of the season and sanity returned to the land after the harvest and vinting. It's at such times that one can smell in the air the decay of a once verdant land, a contrast to the last frigid days of harvesting. The sun spread a warm burnish over the vineyard, illuminating the naked vines so that they took on a bloody red hue against the fading green of the grass in the vineyard alleys. In the distance, Cayuga Lake lay between the long, sloping hills, the water reflecting the darkening blue sky of a diminished day—daylight savings time was now over and the sun would set by five o'clock.

But it was premature to say that the vineyardist was in for a spell of Indian summer. Because the next day called for snow. Perhaps that's why even though such days are work days, they are almost casual work days, in which tasks are done in a kind of anticlimactic repose because the harvest was over and winter would arrive all too soon.

The last major task in the vineyard was hilling up. In one of the alleys of the Chardonnay, Dan sat astride the tractor, looking over his shoulder, then turning and looking ahead to keep his bearing. But it might just as well be Joe in the early years, or John Balliet at King Ferry, or the vineyardists at any of the other wineries around the Finger Lakes. It really doesn't matter who, because it's part of the ritual. Anyway, Dan looked back again at the ridge of dirt peeling up behind the big drive wheel on his right as a steel mold board plow sliced through the soil, turning it so that the crest of earth spilled over and up against the roots of the vines.

The tractor exited the row and swung slowly around to another row two down, retracing the arc of the year before. Dan drove up through it, looking back, looking forward, looking back. The sun began its descent into the southwest.

"The wine is coming along," Gary likes to say at this time of year. But what he really enjoys saying is, "There haven't been any surprises."

Although it was still technically autumn, it looked like winter outside: The Finger Lakes had their first lasting snowfall. Inside the winery, under the fluorescent lights, the barrels sat snugly in their stacked tiers. To all appearances the wine had been put to bed. The most important thing was that it now needed to age. As Alexis, a third-century BC Greek poet, wrote: "Man's nature is not a bit the same as wine's; / He loses flavor as his life declines; / We drink the oldest wine that comes our way; / Old men get nasty, old wines make us gay."

But of course the calm at Long Point Winery was deceptive because always there was the potential of monsters rising from deep within the barrels as the winemaker attempted to capture a fleeting, transient moment in nature.

It's also a time when Gary is inclined to say, "I only wish I had done this ten years earlier."

And now, as the season waned, all Gary could do was nurture the vintage, talk nice to it, silently say a prayer for it, much as winemakers were doing all around the Finger Lakes.

As part of the old ritual Gary stirred the lees once more, then inserted his wine thief into the bunghole to taste, reflect, meditate.

"It's still young. . . . It could be more complex," he said. It was part of the old incantation, attempting to tease meaning from the vintage, some future promise. He moved over to the next barrel, grasped the bung, and removed it. He tasted and nodded silently. Then he inserted the stirring paddle again, and as I watched him row back and forth I had a glimpse of what it was really about: an earnest longing not unlike unrequited love. And as Gary stared into the distance with his gray, luminescent eyes, he looked as if he could be rowing to a land of a winemaker's most earnest dreams and desires.

░▓ ACKNOWLEDGMENTS ▓░

There are many whose assistance in the creation of this book I must acknowledge, not only because of their contributions but also because they joined me on a fascinating journey of discovery. First, I thank my wife and son for their infinite patience as I worked on *Seasons of a Finger Lakes Winery*. Many were the times I would have preferred to be with my family, and I am the poorer for it when I wasn't. Nonetheless, they were always supportive and encouraging. The only constraint my wife placed on me when I began the project was that it be within an hour's drive. But aside from that, she always indulged me, even when I crushed grapes in *her* kitchen, as she insists on calling it. Then, of course, I must express my heartfelt thanks to Gary and Rosemary Barletta for opening their lives to me. They were enthusiastic from the outset, and I only hope that in some small way I have done them justice. I must also acknowledge, of course, Joe Shevaleer and Dan Stevens for instructing me in the ways of the vineyard. They were equally enthusiastic about sharing their knowledge. Then there were so many more whose assistance proved invaluable, such as Russ Nalley, Linda Ehrhart, and Levi Valez-Reed, as well as José Aguilera and his crew. Others whose assistance is greatly appreciated include Pete Saltonstall, John Balliet, Kim Shevaleer, Chris Stamp, Morten Hallgren, Deborah Williams, Bill Nelson of WineAmerica, and the other Bill Nelson, my mapmaker. There were, too, those associated with the Agricultural Experiment Station in Geneva. They include Gavin Sacks, Anna Katharine Mansfield, Tim Martinson, Becky Nelson, and Chris Gerling, as well as cooperative extension agent Hans Walter-Peterson. I would be remiss if I did not also acknowledge Dana Malley, Alice Peters, Jay Wentworth, and Jennifer Coyne. I must also thank my research assistant Andrew Hamilton from SUNY Cortland, for his research on winery licenses and grape varieties grown in the Finger Lakes. I would thank, too, the State University of New York at Cortland where I teach. This project began while I was on sabbatical. I know that must sound like a bit of a scam: I spent my sabbatical at a winery. But the result you hold in your hands.

Then there is my editor, Michael McGandy, and the other Cornell University Press editorial staff whose reading and helpful suggestions likewise proved invaluable. Michael, especially, was indispensable with his recommendations when the manuscript needed a critical look, so that the book very much bears his imprint—assisted when we did flights of wine at Simeon's on rotten winter afternoons in Ithaca.

I also wish to thank my anonymous reviewers for their many helpful suggestions. I would add, too, that often through chance encounters I would meet someone who would contribute some bit of information that became a part of the larger mosaic, such as Erik Bitterbaum who shared his knowledge of bird behavior with me. To those whose names I do not recall, I extend my sincere thanks. If I have left anyone out, I apologize for the frailties of memory.

Finally, I thank my brother, Capt. Peter I. Hartsock, U.S.P.H.S., for always being an encouraging and supportive brother on this project—even though he doesn't drink wine.

John C. Hartsock
Homer, New York

Photographs on pages 39, 144, 180 by Rick Barletta, on pages 58, 65, 132, 168, 172 by Anthony DeRado, and on pages 8, 13, 61, 113 by Dan Stevens. Photographs on pages 85, 152 by the author.

SUGGESTED READINGS

In my research on wine, I found many useful books. For those who may have an interest in learning more about wine and its making, I suggest the following. Everybody seemed to recommend Jancis Robinson's *Oxford Companion to Wine* as the bible of wine literature, and it is truly as all-encompassing an examination of enology and viticulture as I have found, while remaining reasonably accessible. For those who wish to focus on learning how to taste wine, a helpful book is Ed McCarthy's and Mary Ewing-Mulligan's *Wine for Dummies*. Two with a focus on the geography of winemaking are Oz Clarke's *The Essential Wine Book,* and Hugh Johnson's and Jancis Robinson's *The World of Wine*. For those interested in making wine at home, I suggest Jon Iverson's *Home Winemaking Step by Step*. For grape growing there is the American Wine Society's *Growing Wine Grapes*.

My research took me into the history of wine as a cultural phenomenon. Among books of that nature, I can recommend Rod Phillips's *A Short History of Wine,* and Paul Lukacs's *American Vintage: The Rise of American Wine*. For those interested in the famous 1976 wine tasting in Paris where California wines won first place to the surprise of many, thus establishing the reputation of American wines, I recommend *Judgment of Paris* by George M. Taber. Then, for understanding the ancient history of wine, I direct readers to Patrick E. McGovern's *Ancient Wine*. Finally, a book long out of print but which you may still find on the library bookshelves is William Younger's *Gods, Men, and Wine*. While the information can be dated, it nonetheless provides a delicious examination of the place of wine in our civilization.